MY SABER IS BENT

JACK PAAR

INTRODUCTION BY ALEXANDER KING

ILLUSTRATED WITH
16 PAGES OF PHOTOGRAPHS

A GIANT CARDINAL EDITION published by
POCKET BOOKS, INC. • NEW YORK

MY SABER IS BENT

Trident Press edition published December, 1961

Giant Cardinal edition published December, 1962
1st printing........October, 1962

This *Giant Cardinal*** edition includes every word contained in the
original, higher-priced edition. It is printed from brand-new
plates made from completely reset, clear, easy-to-read type.
Giant Cardinal editions are published by Pocket Books, Inc., and
are printed and distributed in the U.S.A. by Affiliated Publishers,
a division of Pocket Books, Inc., 630 Fifth Avenue, New York 20, N.Y.
*Trademark registered in the United States and other countries.
**Trademark of Pocket Books, Inc., 630 Fifth
Avenue, New York 20, N.Y., in the United States
and other countries.

L

Contents

v

vi • *Contents*

A Word to the Wise Guys

FOR ALMOST A YEAR now I have been toying with the notion of writing a short piece about Jack Paar. I was going to call it "Voyage Around Paar" because I am convinced that it is practically impossible to write a truly objectively revealing article about any person that you go on seeing with comparative frequency. Just think how difficult it would be to give a fair and dispassionate account of one's wife or husband, for instance, and yet you might imagine that the ultimate intimacies of matrimony would be particularly helpful in such an appraisal.

Not so at all.

Successful biographies prosper most effectively upon graves, since, if the subject of your text is still at liberty and floating around, he seems forever ready and eager to contradict your most carefully documented and cogently summarized conclusions about him.

Nevertheless, I have decided to take my chance and try to put down at least a fleeting vignette on this already overly publicized, nocturnal biped.

First of all, I don't think you can even begin to write about Paar without taking a careful gander at the unique framework within which his highly peculiar activities take place. Now then, before I say anything about television in general, let me give you a little analytical breakdown on the special mystique which activates *The Jack Paar Show*.

Believe me, I have thought a good deal about this, and you can take my word for it that *The Jack Paar Show* is something that has accrued around Jack exactly as the snail-shell eventually accumulates around the snail. The style, the format and the contents of this entertainment tidbit are chemically and psychologically composed of all Jack's virtues, his animadversions, his prejudices and his failings. In its totality it represents a most uniquely personal triumph in a medium in which predigested mincemeat, warmed-over hash and the other unidentifiable mish-mash which derives from group cooking furnishes the steady diet for a practically indifferent public.

As a matter of fact, even his niggling belittlers have to concede that there could be no *Paar Show,* in its presently bewildering orbit, if Jack Paar wasn't there to keep it spinning. There could be no such show for the simple reason that Jack has sweated the whole damned thing right out of his highly mercurial, endlessly multifaceted personality. His nightly offering on N.B.C. provides an extraordinary manifestation in the television field, particularly if you consider that this show is the only one which, in five years of steady and undeniable TV decline, has maintained a constantly rising graph of intrinsic entertainment merit.

So what does Jack Paar actually do on that show of his?

I'll tell you what he does. He somehow manages to distill the most worthwhile aspects of the TV medium into the most flexible form of unrehearsed, adult entertainment. He does a nightly verbal striptease in the company of some of the most articulate and amusing people in the country, and the public, almost completely stultified by the hodge-podge that is usually slopped onto its home screens, is only too eager to stay up until all hours of the morning to participate joyfully in this unpredictable charade.

Year after year we have all of us seen the great movie and theatrical stars performing their artistic chores in their carefully prescribed roles, but only on the Paar show do they finally achieve any sort of human identity at all. It is only on *The Jack Paar Show* that Suzy Parker emerges as the citizen next door and is quite free to display her unglamorous concerns with everyday life, a life which ordinarily receives only its gossipy overtones in the waspish columns of the daily papers. Indeed, it is only on the Paar program that Mr. James Cagney is at liberty to quote a poem by Emily Dickinson and Peter Ustinov can recount some of his most hilarious war experiences.

Where else?

The show has other virtues, too, of course. It has cleared the paths for a lot of talent and made the way easy for people with remarkable gifts to place their accomplishments before the public.

But I think its truly unique contribution to TV, and one that can only be identified with Jack's own peculiar aptitudes, lies in the fact that people with rich lives and lively imaginations have suddenly found themselves able to display their unique attributes in an atmosphere of *almost unlimited freedom.*

Another thing: because Jack is so completely involved with the show—not only as an *entrepreneur,* but as a deeply active participant—the whole production suffers an instant organic blow the moment he doesn't appear on it. That's just common sense, isn't it?

Let me tell you a little something about that.

You see, the actors and various professional entertainers who appear as his guests have, mostly, only two or three stories to offer on the altar of split-second improvisation. Anyone who knows actors at all will tell you that most of them aren't really much good without a memorized script. Only the highly exceptional ones among them can draw on a wide enough variety of experiences to be granted a free passage to those dangerous precincts where swift verbalization is expected as a matter of course. Well then, let me tell you that Jack has an absolutely uncanny faculty for guessing the approach of the exhaustion point on the part of his guests, and, by an adroitness that has become second nature to him, he

manages, almost miraculously, to steer them into the less tur-
bulent areas of more generalized conversation (or steer them
offstage altogether). To do this without embarrassment to
your visitor—to do it so that it sometimes seems that it is the
host who is fumbling around in waters too shallow for his
navigation—therein, I say, lies some of the great, undercover
skill of a truly great professional interlocutor.

All this has been going on for nearly five years, right now,
and, what is more, I sincerely believe the show is getting better all the time. Jack is a quick-witted hombre with an absolutely fabulous memory. He has, of course, the instant appeal
of his considerable good looks, as well as his carefully fostered midwestern awkwardness, which make him so irresistible a fetish for middle-aged ladies of all sorts. I say *carefully
fostered* because I think it is an attitude he feels is highly
consonant with the public image that is best suited to his personality. He is certainly quite genuinely square about some
things, but he is fully aware of it and sees no reason to amelio-
rate it as long as it is good for the show.

Actually, he has proven, over the years, to be one of the
least hypocritical of men, and I can vouch that he is quite
free from any sort of misleading or evasive pretenses. Why
should he bother? After all, he has *made* it absolutely on his
own terms; hasn't he?

Even if you are only vaguely familiar with show business, I
hope you realize what a truly stupendous statement has just
been made. I said, "He has *made it absolutely on his own
terms.*"

There is no success in the world which can be achieved on
a higher level.

For Jack's many envious detractors who believe, or pretend
to believe, that he is just a very lucky guy, without a shred of
talent, I offer the following little parable.

Once upon a time, in the ancient kingdom of Persia, the
Shah established a rest home for some of his superannuated

camp followers. In one room of this quiet retreat there were six beds placed along the wall, and, since there was only a single window at the end of this chamber, it naturally came about that the pensioner placed nearest to the window was the only one who had a view of the colorful world which still went on about its business, on the outside.

And so it happened that this man, whose name was Dschafar, would for many hours each day keep the rest of the inmates informed about the lively things that took place beneath that window. He never seemed to weary in describing the various people who passed on their way to the market place: the soldiers, the merchants and the many seductive women who jiggled their undulant curves while pursuing their multitudinous errands in the street below. Lacking such subjects, Dschafar would, from time to time, expatiate at length on the many changes that he observed in the aspects of nature as they occurred in the gardens across the way, and by suchlike discourses he made the other members of the dormitory forget, for a time at least, that their own active days on this earth were almost over.

"The fledgling swallows in that almond tree," he said, "have taken their first flight this morning. Their parents are flitting with pride and anxiety all around them."

At another time he said, "That milkmaid in the pale blue scarf has had a letter of good news today, and all day long she walked about her duties like a queen."

Now then, the man who lay prone on his back in the bed next to Dschafar's was a man called Mirza, and, after a while, this man became extremely envious of Dschafar. He couldn't bear the thought that all the riches and splendors of the world should be spread out so freely right outside their chamber, and that no one really had access to them excepting his fortunate neighbor. This envy eventually turned Mirza's heart to bitter hatred against Dschafar, and finally the wretched man even decided to kill the chronic blabberer, and perhaps obtain the use of the one bed that allowed a view of the city beyond the rest-house walls.

And this he did.

Through a visiting friend he managed to obtain a quantity of some particularly virulent poison, and, while the unsuspecting Dschafar was soundly asleep, Mirza poured this evil thing into his neighbor's tea.

The following day Dschafar was dead, and the secretly rejoicing Mirza was promptly moved into his place.

And then, when at last Mirza raised himself on one elbow and looked eagerly out of the window, he beheld only a barren field that seemed to reach as far off as the horizon. Mirza blinked his eyes like a man bereft of his senses and frantically clutched at his bedposts.

There was nothing to see—nothing but a desolation of bare ground and grayish rubble and a bit of dirty paper blown fitfully about by the evening wind.

With a great cry Mirza fell back upon his pillow, for he suddenly realized that all those lovely visions beyond that window had only existed in Dschafar's mind.

—ALEXANDER KING

Preface

THE LITERARY FOLKS are up in arms lately about something they call non-books. A non-book, according to *Time* magazine, is something written by non-authors for non-people.

H. Allen Smith, the humorist, and other authors and critics have also taken up the hue and cry against the invasion of the literary pastures by retired boxers, clergymen, reformed alcoholics and even entertainers, who have taken to writing books, usually in collaboration with professional writers.

As a guilty member of this motley crew, having committed a book called *I Kid You Not* in 1960, I would like to make a few comments on assorted other nons including non-reading critics, literary nonentities and other nonsense.

When I was dragooned into becoming an author of sorts, I protested that I didn't fancy myself as a potential Dickens, Tolstoi or even Louisa May Alcott or Zane Grey. Although I'd sold a story to a national magazine when I was twenty-two, I had no intention of writing a book until I was seduced into it under the influence of flattery and money.

A good while before *Time* got around to it, I pointed out in my book that authorship was getting as contagious as mumps and that practically everyone was turning writer.

"Rock n' roll singers, ladies who disrobe in public, former streetcar conductors and female discus throwers are all penning their lives," I warned. "Young people are writing their autobiographies before there has been time for anything to happen."

One publisher, I discovered, had five hundred kids locked

in a room writing a book called *Art Linkletter Says the Darndest Things.*

Although I approached my literary debut lightheartedly, *Time* and various critics registered alarm at the idea of books being written by anyone but dyed-in-the-wool, 32-carat, bona fide genius type writers. While I scarcely felt that Sir Cedric Hardwicke, Billy Graham, Barry Goldwater or I were threats to Ernest Hemingway or Somerset Maugham, I did feel that a great many people other than professional writers might have dramatic or amusing stories to tell.

I felt that Dr. Tom Dooley, the dedicated young man who devoted himself to saving lives in the jungles of Laos, and then died of cancer, had a more absorbing story than some smiling, wavy-haired fictional hero created by a real honest-to-goodness writer. And I'd just as soon curl up with Zsa Zsa Gabor, even in book form, as with the fictional Madame Bovary. After all, Sheila Graham, in whose arms he died, has shed as revealing a light on the tragic F. Scott Fitzgerald, even with the assistance of a collaborator, as the many genuine writers who have picked over his literary bones.

My feelings on this score were borne out, I felt, when *I Kid You Not* attained the number two spot among the non-fiction best sellers, despite the hoots or silence of most of the critics. Even though no New York paper mentioned the book, except for a couple of uncomplimentary lines in one sheet, it sold over two hundred thousand copies in hard-covers and more than one million as a paperback—which gives some indication of the influence critics have on the sale of a book.

Most of the papers that ran reviews reviewed *me* instead of the book. One began, "Jack Paar has written his autobiography. Ho hum." Right away I began to get the feeling that that review wouldn't be entirely objective.

The attitude of the critics generally reminded me of the critic who, when asked if he had read a certain author, replied, "Something that I once wrote about him prejudiced me so that I was never able to read him."

The main objection of critics seems to be the use of a collaborator in writing a book. However, I fail to see anything reprehensible in someone whose chief occupation is preaching, weight-lifting, being President of the United States or performing on television getting some assistance in writing his story.

I didn't want to overdo this form of literary liaison, so I got a collaborator who had never written a book either. He is my friend John Reddy of the *Reader's Digest*. John used to specialize in writing about Most Unforgettable Characters but he had to give that up because he couldn't remember them. I talked into a dictaphone and John typed, putting in commas and paragraphs and giving first aid to the split infinitives.

For some reason, critics look with horror on the dictaphone as a literary tool. They don't seem to accept anyone as an author unless he sits down and pecks out every word on a typewriter, which I also do, but slowly and badly. Because of this, I usually prefer talking a story to typing it and feel no special admiration for authors simply because they type, as many of them seem to be better typists than writers.

I don't see what difference it makes, so long as you have something to say. Writers, I feel, are merely people with ideas and stories to tell. Schiller, the German poet, sometimes wrote sitting on a piece of ice. Thomas Wolfe wrote standing up, with his tablet on top of a refrigerator. My friend Alex King writes on a breadboard and he has made more money that way than anyone since the National Biscuit Company. And Winston Churchill dictates sitting in bed. Strictly a non-writer type.

I usually use a tape recorder. I like to tell stories but I never did have any ambition to write those illuminated manuscripts like the monks in the Middle Ages.

The way the literary people carry on, you'd think that writing was solely the province of inspired geniuses toiling lovingly over each gemlike word in utter solitude. Actually, as Cameron Shipp pointed out, Moses was the first "as-told-to" writer and literary creation has frequently been a matter of collaboration dating back to the Bible—one of the biggest writing collaborations of all time.

Although Solomon, Daniel, Isaiah, Matthew, Mark, Luke, John and dozens of others got name credit in the good book, no one knows how many unknown writers—they didn't call them ghosts in those days—had a hand in it. The King James version alone required fifty-four translators, and if you don't think they were a ghostly lot try to name one. Don't start with King James. He just called the meeting to order.

The Constitution of the United States, which Gladstone called "the most wonderful work ever struck off at a given time by the brain and purpose of man," was the work of thirty-seven men in Philadelphia on a hot summer in 1787.

So it goes. Nobody seems sure who wrote Shakespeare; Marlowe and Bacon are among those suspected of having ghosted the works of the Bard. Alexander Dumas is reported to have had more writers than Bob Hope, toiling away in obscurity over his famous books.

Some of the best known books have been through more hands than a chain letter. I was a little disillusioned to learn that the *Encyclopaedia Britannica* is the work of thousands of authors and not one sterling, honest-to-goodness writer named Joe Brittanica. And how about that best seller, the *Betty Crocker Cook Book?*

Do you think that Betty Crocker makes up all those recipes out of her pretty little head? Well, Virginia, I hate to be the one to break the news, but there is no real live Betty Crocker. She is not only a non-writer; she is a non-person.

I've never felt the same about her pineapple upside-down cake since.

Another thing that annoys me is the implication that book-writing was real literature until it was invaded by us part-time authors, and that until the invention of the tape recorder and Gerold Frank everyone sat around reading Dante in the original and wondering what Lord Byron was really like. Well, I've done a little checking up on that score, too.

During the sixty years between 1895 and 1955, the fifteen best sellers in this country included nine novels, three inspirational books, two cookbooks and one baby book. Of the nine that made this best seller list, seven were by Mickey Spillane. Mr. Spillane, of course, is a genuine writer who personally writes every pistol shot in the belly and roll in the hay.

Since professional writers have criticized the methods of sometime writers like myself, I've been observing their methods to see if perhaps I couldn't pick up a few pointers. The only good literary advice I ever heard was that offered by Thomas Wolfe to a student who asked him what kind of writing to do. "Always write masterpieces," Wolfe advised. "There's a better market for them."

However, there seems to be a considerable dearth of masterpieces these days, even among genuine writers. Although they criticize the technique of dictating a book as beneath them, true, painstaking craftsmen all, some of them seem to grind them out in an awful hurry. H. Allen Smith, a leading complainer against non-writers, has just written his twenty-fifth book.

Yet he's a mere piker compared to Georges Simenon, a mystery writer, who reels off about ten books a year and had written one hundred and twenty-five at last count. (This does not include any he's finished in the last ten minutes.)

I suppose the professional writers have a point in resenting this wholesale invasion by people who don't write for a living. In a way I can sympathize with H. Allen Smith when he says, "I object to being pushed off the best seller list by some doctor from Vermont."

Yet while we non-literary types have been invading the ranks of writers, the authors and critics have been swarming into the entertainment business at an appalling rate. I'm not speaking of authors who turn up on shows like ours to plug their latest books. What I mean is writers who turn up on TV making like entertainers.

I don't think they tell jokes any better than they think I write books.

It seems like every time I turn on television lately some author is impersonating an entertainer. Every time I look, there is Bennett Cerf or Clifton Fadiman or Cleveland Amory on the screen. Several authors have even turned up with their own shows. Ben Hecht had his own show for a while. So did Fannie Hurst, another author.

John Gunther, who wrote *Inside Europe, Inside Asia* and other "inside" books, also has a show. I haven't seen it but, knowing his penchant for looking inside places, I assume it's on X ray rather than TV.

Since authors have no qualms about invading show business, I have no trepidation about turning author. When I think of some of the books I've read, by genuine writers bearing the Clifton Fadiman Seal of Approval, I am reminded of Joe Frisco's observation when he proposed teaming up with another vaudevillian.

"I've s-s-seen your act," said Joe, "and I c-c-can't hurt it."

Robert Morley, one of the world's great conversationalists, once said, "Show business is quite simple. You tell the audience *what* you are going to do. Then you *do* it. After that, you tell them that you've *done* it."

So you have now been told that I am now going to write another book.

—JACK PAAR

MY SABER IS BENT

1

Paar's Law

WHILE BROWSING through Nick Kenny's column one day, in a fit of masochism, I discovered that Vincent Lopez, the orchestra leader and amateur astrologist, had cast my horoscope. Considering that he missed the correct date of my birthday by a week, the veteran music-maker and numerologist seemed to have done a pretty good job of analyzing my character.

Pointing out that I was born under the sign of Taurus, the Bull, and that my ruling planet is Venus, Lopez wrote that I was "stubborn, inclined to go off half-cocked and regret it later, and just plain unreasonable." That's me, all right.

However, on reading further, I discovered that the same also applies to Queen Elizabeth, Bing Crosby, Kate Smith and Fred Astaire, all of whom were likewise born under the sign of Taurus.

Warming to his work, Lopez got down to particulars. "Jack Paar will find many balls of fire that he started to roll last year unfolding in 1961," he predicted. "A year of a lot of restlessness and uncertainty of decisions, which he should not make until after September twenty-third."

Now he tells me. He waits until May to tell me not to make any decisions until September twenty-third. Lopez just sat by and let me muddle through January, February, March and April before issuing his warning, and there I was making decisions right and left every day and hardly giving it a thought. Already I had made hundreds of decisions, including one to

1

break my old Vincent Lopez recording of *Dardanella,* and suddenly he cautions me not to decide anything until fall.

Well, his warning came too late. The trouble was that I had already decided on January second to write this book. While other people were nursing hangovers, breaking their New Year's resolutions or just out on the highway running up the holiday accident toll, I began writing this tome, which may be an accident of another sort. But that's the story of my life. People always warn me when it's too late.

It's all the inexorable working of what I call Paar's Law. Paar's Law, which I formulated after years of misadventures, is that if there's any trouble around, it will seek me out. I seem to attract trouble like blue serge attracts lint. It's not that I deliberately hunt it out. I just seem to have a knack for backing into it. If I cross the street to avoid trouble, I get arrested for jaywalking.

Of late my propensity for attracting trouble seems to have become global in scope. I met with Fidel Castro and we broke off diplomatic relations with him. I went to Berlin and it became an incident. I announced I was going to Russia and Khrushchev resumed nuclear testing. Maybe it's only coincidental, but it looks like Paar's Law to me.

I've been blamed for a lot of things since taking over our nightly exercise in group therapy. Cleveland Amory says I helped kill Society. Curt Weinberg, the owner of the *Blue Angel* in New York, says our show killed the big time night-club business.

"I'll tell you what killed the night-club business in New York —Jack Paar," he told columnist Paul Molloy. "This one guy is the reason why clubs are dying all over the place."

And a worried mother wrote to "Dear Abby," the columnist, saying that she watched me so much while she was pregnant that her baby looks and acts exactly like me. Poor baby. But things might have been worse. It's a good thing she wasn't watching Huntley and Brinkley, or she might have had twins.

For years I have suffered from a chronic case of *orpetope-*

dalogy or foot-in-mouth disease. "Why do I get in so much trouble?" I once asked Hugh Downs. "Is it my big mouth?"

"No," said Hugh. "It's just that you're utterly and instantly frank and . . . well, yes, it *is* your big mouth."

My whole life has been as disorderly as a Kiddie Matinee at a neighborhood movie, and straightening me out seems as hopeless as unscrambling an egg. Even the little things go wrong.

If I go out with an umbrella it never rains, but if I wash the car it's sure to pour. My ballpoint pen never starts writing when I do, and when I go through a turnstile it gets fresh with me. If I try something simple like shaking the catsup out of the bottle I emerge looking like a wounded Indian.

It's the same with television. My show has been the scene of so much controversy that it's now televised in living color —black and blue. It's gotten so that some of my best friends are enemies.

I bear the marks of this conflict and what appears to be my smart, Ivy League suit is actually scar tissue, beautifully tailored. I've suffered so many vicissitudes in television that some of my friends have petitioned Washington to have me declared a disaster area.

I make no attempt to understand it. It's just the mysterious working of Paar's Law.

Much of the confusion which attends my existence seems to crop up on the domestic front. I don't know why it is that merely eluding the booby traps of day-to-day existence is so difficult, and that the path of simple domesticity at times seems strewn with land mines.

Some years ago, when we lived in Hollywood, where I was in bondage to a studio, we acquired a housekeeper. She was a wonderful soul, cheerful and efficient, but she had one vice—she played the races. I don't know what her system was —I suspect it was based on voodoo—but it was remarkably ineffective. Not content with trying unsuccessfully to beat the ponies at Santa Anita and Hollywood Park, she took to borrowing money from Miriam, my wife, to enlarge her operations.

Even that wasn't so bad, but she began to absent herself from her domestic chores with increasing frequency as her efforts to recoup her losses became more frenzied. We always got the bad news that she wouldn't be in from her husband, an amiable man with an imaginative turn of mind in thinking up alibis.

"Mary won't be able to come in today, Mr. Paar," he would announce dolefully on the phone. "She had an operation—for appendicitis."

The fact that Mary would turn up the next day exuding more good health than Vic Tanny, and with no mention of an operation, never seemed to daunt either one of them. These ailments and operations, moreover, always seemed to coincide with an important race at one of the big tracks.

Also, these imaginary maladies never had any lasting effect. Once she reportedly had "her tonsils out," although I noticed her drinking steaming soup with gusto the next day. Another time she allegedly "broke her ankle." Two days later she was wheeling Randy around the block and apparently not hurting anyplace but in the pocketbook.

We liked her so much we never complained, and, too, we got a vicarious kick out of our contributions to Mary's deficit financing system of betting.

One day, however, Mary's husband called and reported, again, that she would be unable to come in.

"Oh, that's too bad," I said sympathetically. "What's the trouble?"

There was a pregnant silence. I could tell that her husband either hadn't thought of a good alibi this time, or had run through all the diseases he knew.

"She had to go to New York," he said finally. "On business."

My ineptitude seems to be contagious and of late even Miriam is showing a talent for bumbling her way into awkward situations. This is odd because in the past she has always been a model of brisk proficiency and has gone about her daily rounds in a manner so well organized as to be downright unnerving. With Miriam a trip to the neighborhood supermarket is as highly coordinated as the Allied invasion plan on D-Day, and a shopping list is made out with a meticulous care usually lavished only on projects like shooting a man into space.

I long ago abandoned trying to remember anyone's name in the argle-bargle of meeting a group of strangers, but Miriam always recalls everyone's name by an efficient system of word association. However, recently Paar's Law seems to be affecting her, too.

Not long ago we attended a dinner party at the home of Jerry Danzig, one of N.B.C.'s innumerable vice presidents. One of the guests was Orvil Dryfoos, the publisher of *The New York Times*. While I mumbled greetings to Mr. Dryfoos, Miriam said with her usual efficiency, "Excuse me, I didn't quite catch your name."

"It's Dryfoos . . . Orvil Dryfoos," repeated the publisher.

"Oh, of course," said Miriam. "Orvil, like Orville Wright."

During dinner, while I tried valiantly but unavailingly to remember the names of the guests on either side of me, I brooded darkly over Miriam's system for recalling names by association.

However, as we were taking our leave, Miriam shook hands with Mr. Dryfoos and said in her most winning manner, "It was so nice to meet you, Wilbur."

The inexplicable working of Paar's Law has complicated not only our domestic life but sometimes intrudes upon the show, confusing my finest hour and three-quarters.

When I took over the show on July 29, 1957, it followed a disaster called *America After Dark* which ranks high, I am told by connoisseurs of such matters, among TV's alltime darkest hours. To my surprise, as much as anyone's, our modest, low budget display of violent informality became a hit.

Before long I was reading that N.B.C. was harvesting millions from the program. This pleased me as much as it must have surprised N.B.C., and I certainly felt that they didn't owe me anything beyond what they were paying me. However, I began to get what I thought were little hints that the network planned to present me with some little surprise token of appreciation for the success the show had achieved. These subtle indications began to multiply as the program's first anniversary neared.

I had been thinking of buying a Chevrolet Corvette and one day I mentioned this to my producer.

"I wouldn't buy one if I were you," he said, rather pointedly I thought. I took this to be an indication that the network might be getting the car for me. My suspicions that this might be the case increased as the date of the anniversary approached. In fact, the night of the anniversary the producer asked me not to go backstage before the show as they had a little surprise planned.

During the show they sprang the surprise. While the orchestra played *Happy Birthday*, the curtains parted dramatically. There stood no shiny new Corvette, as I had anticipated, but a motley group of my "best friends," including several I didn't even recognize.

They wanted to surprise me—and they certainly did!

My mother, a nice but misguided lady, always hoped that I'd be a minister when I grew up. Happily religion was spared this disaster, but it wasn't my mother's fault. When I was a little boy she used to read the Bible to me, and when I got bigger she gave me a bible. Other people gave me bibles too, and before long it seemed as though I had more bibles than the Commodore Hotel.

I grew to love the Bible, but I never became a member of

any religious denomination. However, people keep trying to convert me. My mother has never given up hope, and now Miriam and Randy, our daughter, have joined in the campaign. People I don't even know write to assure me there is hope for even the worst sinner, and that they are praying for me. For years Billy Graham, the eminent evangelist, has been trying to convert me, and has forcibly led me to church on occasions, but with no lasting results.

Now George Jessel seems to be trying. He keeps bombarding me with bibles. Jessel's interest in my spiritual welfare first manifested itself sometime ago in Hollywood. He called enthusiastically one day to tell me he had a friend who wanted to present me with a bible on the program. I was touched by this generous thought and assumed it was some clergyman or possibly one of the devout ladies who write that they have been praying for me. It turned out, however, to be Beverly Aadland, the pretty, teen-aged friend of the late Errol Flynn.

Miss Aadland had become enmeshed in some bizarre, front-page difficulties, after the death of Flynn, and a California court had placed her under the supervision of a minister. This had turned her to religion, Jessel explained, and she felt it had done so much for her she wanted to give me some.

I wasn't sure that this was exactly a compliment, and anyway I already had a plethora of bibles. I admitted to Jessel that I could stand a little uplifting, but I wasn't sure that Beverly Aadland was the one to lead me down the path of rectitude.

I suggested that the idea of a sixteen-year-old night-club entertainer, who had been involved in a variety of colorful escapades, making a public presentation of a bible on TV was ludicrous, and might set the cause of religion back further than anything short of my conversion.

As a result, Beverly demurely gave me the bible in private. It was a large, handsome King James Version, and was warmly inscribed by Miss Aadland herself.

Immediately the bible presented a problem. For one thing, since I already had numerous bibles, I saw no reason to carry another one three thousand miles to New York. Moreover, I was flying back and the bible wouldn't fit in my luggage.

What to do? I could leave it in my hotel suite but it, too, already had a bible. Also, it wouldn't do to leave a bible winningly autographed by Beverly Aadland just lying around like that. People might get ideas.

I experimented with hiding it under the mattress, but it made a lump about the size of second base in the middle of the bed. I was aware that a religious object should be disposed of by burning, but I didn't think Conrad Hilton would appreciate my building a bonfire in one of his best suites. I suddenly began to feel panicky and then I realized.

It was Paar's Law operating again.

Finally, in desperation, I managed to squeeze my hot bible into my suitcase by giving a pair of nearly new shoes to the bellhop.

When I got back to New York I still didn't know what to do with the bible. I finally gave it to my mother, who was delighted to get it. She explained she had given me her last bible some years before.

The bible presentation in California, it developed, was just the opening shot in a continuous barrage by George Jessel, aimed at keeping me supplied with religious inspiration. Ever since, he has been showering me with more bibles and other religious objects.

One night he came on the program, just back from an Israeli Bond tour on which he said he "had left no Cohen unturned." First, he presented me with a George Jessel Bar Mitzvah kit, which contained a yamilke and other objects used in the Jewish confirmation. He then presented me with an album of Israeli songs he had recorded.

Tom Cochran, my associate producer, was watching this display of generosity from backstage with a slightly jaundiced eye, since each object Georgie handed me bore the Jessel name.

"Finally," George continued, "for Randy I have this beautiful copy of the Old Testament. . . ."

"As told to George Jessel," cracked Cochran from the wings.

But of all the things I have become involved in through the mysterious working of Paar's Law, none was more baffling than my investigation by Congress.

Now there's a status symbol! Sometimes when I'm with people, and the conversation seems to be lagging, I casually toss off, "Well, the time I was investigated by the Harris Committee . . ."

I tell you, it's a conversation stopper.

Actually, being investigated by Congress is rather an eerie experience. Nothing much seems to happen, and if it does you're the last to know. I had always envisioned it as sitting under the hot lights, like Frank Costello before the Kefauver Committee, in front of a row of hard-eyed legislators looking like the panel on *What's My Line?*

Well, it doesn't work that way.

My brush with our lawmakers began quite innocently when I bought a lot on Key Biscayne, Florida, a beautiful, quiet little island, just far enough removed from the gaudy pleasure domes of Miami Beach. The price of the lot was $37,500. I paid $1,000 down and was planning on paying the balance in installments.

One night I showed a brief film of the lot on our TV show and told how I hoped to retire there someday, if I could ever afford it. The next thing I knew I was being investigated by Congress, just as if I were some big issue like the Cost-of-Living or Un-American Affairs.

The House Subcommittee on Legislative Oversight, headed by Representative Oren Harris of Arkansas, demanded a tape of the show, so it could scrutinize my mention of the lot. The committee said it was going to track down whether I was getting the property free, or at a rakeoff, as payola in return for the TV plug.

Shortly before, Congressman Harris had struck publicity paydirt when he trapped Presidential-aide Sherman Adams with a vicuna coat and a Persian rug which he had accepted from Bernard Goldfine, the sometime philanthropist. He nabbed Dick Clark, too, for taking gifts for playing songs like "Splish, Splash" and "Itsy Bitsy Teeny Weeny Yellow Polka Dot Bikini" on his TV show, and also Charles Van Doren and other fixed quiz winners as they were fleeing their isolation booths with their ill-gotten gains.

You don't catch public enemies like Dick Clark every day, and I think the Congressman was getting a little restless for more publicity, so he decided to find out whether I was up to any skulduggery in Florida.

Although the committee described the investigation as routine, and said no conclusions were to be attached to it, the newspapers splashed the announcement of the probe in large type. The first I knew of the whole ruckus was when I saw it on the front pages in Tokyo, enroute from Hong Kong where I fled after my celebrated joke about a water closet.

When I got back to this country I found it on the front pages here, too. I turned over all my papers and cancelled checks to the N.B.C. lawyers and told them I would be happy to appear before the committee.

I had just one comment when reporters asked me what I had to say about the accusation. I said that I had bought the lot and was paying for it just like anyone else. Then I added that I hoped the committee and the newspapers would tell the *outcome* of the investigation just as prominently as they were featuring the *beginning*.

I never did find out what happened when the committee saw the film. Did they think there were too many commercials? Did Congressman Harris like Charley Weaver's "Letter from Mama"? Could they understand Geneviève's accent? I never got a clue.

Weeks went by and I never heard a word. I kept waiting for the other shoe to drop, but it never did.

I have nothing against Congressional committees investigating anything or anybody. In fact, I was eager to testify. It was just the cloak-and-dagger methods that annoyed me; the big splurge of headlines and then silence.

The committee concluded its TV hearings without ever either calling or clearing me. There was just the flurry of stories about their investigating me, and then silence.

Finally a committee member mentioned in an offhand way that the investigation had been dropped. When he did, the newspapers buried it in a few lines back somewhere between the obituaries and Dick Tracy. By this time I was getting used to such strange goings-on.

It was just Paar's Law.

In 1960 I made a sentimental journey back to Hollywood. I had departed the film capital nearly ten years before, unemployed and dejected, feeling, as Jean Kerr once said of an actor in similar circumstances, "like the sinking ship leaving the rats."

Now I was coming back a success. Hollywood had inscribed my name among the screen immortals in its sidewalk. My name, I was told, was accorded a place of honor on the sidewalk of Hollywood Boulevard along with such movie luminaries as Rudolph Valentino, Helen Twelvetrees, Pola Negri, Sonny Tufts, Rod LaRoque, Nita Naldi and the Dead End Kids.

I was quite touched at this recognition of a prodigal son as, to tell the truth, I never made much of a dent on Hollywood and often had difficulty coping with its folkways.

I had been summoned to Hollywood by R.K.O. Studios

shortly after returning from the South Pacific at the end of World War II. As is customary in the film capital, the studio decided to make me over—at least in a few places. They capped my teeth and decided my hair should be thicker. They announced they were going to outfit me with a hairpiece to give me a widow's peak.

I grudgingly submitted to trying out this hirsute bonus. However, I began to suspect the studio wasn't thinking in large terms about my prospects when I discovered that the hairpiece with which they equipped me was no glorious profusion of hair, fresh from the hand of Max Factor, but a second-hand one that had once adorned the head of Zachary Scott.

I made a few pictures at R.K.O. and 20th Century-Fox, but even with my shiny capped teeth, courtesy of Howard Hughes, and Zachary Scott's erstwhile hairpiece, I never made much of a splash in movies. I remained as anonymous as David Susskind's associates in Talent Associates and there was a conspicuous lack of mourning among the studios when I departed Lotus Land for the East.

As a result it felt good to be coming back to see my name embedded in the sidewalk along with those of all the famous movie stars. It was quite a search but Miriam and I finally found it. There it was on Hollywood Boulevard, a big star in the sidewalk and my name.

It was a strange feeling to look down and see my own name in concrete, surrounded by those of famous actors. Then I took a closer look. They'd misspelled it! Also, it was under the canopy of a mortuary.

"Isn't that nice, dear," said Miriam, ever the positive thinker. "At least you're in the shade."

There it was—Paar's Law all over again.

So if anyone knows of a Jack Parr (with two r's instead of two a's), who might be needing a tombstone soon, I might be able to get him a real buy. I don't know what Hollywood plans to do about its little *faux pas*. Maybe they'll have to move my slab to a busy intersection, so the buses can erase it.

But I'm not upset about the mistake. It's just one of those things that sometimes go wrong in Hollywood—like the weather. But if they can't spell Paar right, what will happen when they get to Gina Lollobrigida?

2

What Have You Done for Me Lately?

ONE SPRING EVENING, after finishing our show, I was making
my usual furtive escape from N.B.C.'s Radio City, or Rodeo
City as it is now sometimes called since the network has been
showing so many westerns. It had been one of those days. I
woke up early and couldn't get back to sleep. I had installed a
new television set and couldn't get anything on it except what
seemed to be a snowstorm. Things hadn't gone well on the
show. I'd fouled up a couple of commercials and a face-cream
sponsor was reported threatening to commit suicide by jumping into a vat of his own product and softening to death. So
I was happy to be escaping into the pleasant spring night.

As soon as I got off the elevator, I saw the usual little clump
of autograph seekers lying in ambush. I loath giving auto-
graphs, since I have never been able to figure out what people
do with them, so I took evasive action. Calling to José Melis
to follow me, I bolted out of the elevator and burst through
the little knot of adenoidal teenagers and adult delinquents
who were drawn up with pens and paper poised.

José and I were gradually outfooting our pursuers in the
chase down the corridors, when out of the corner of my eye
I saw that one of them was a little old lady in a flowered hat
and thick glasses. I was struck by an immediate pang of conscience and skidded to a stop. The other pursuers closed in,
too, but I said, "Sorry, just the lady."

She handed me a paper and I quickly scribbled my signa-
ture. She looked at me gratefully and said, "Thank you *so*

much, Mr. Paar." Then she smilingly pressed an envelope in my hand.

I stuffed the envelope in my pocket and resumed my flight with José to our car. Then, as we pulled away, I opened the envelope. It was a summons.

That incident served to remind me once again that good intentions often have the quality of boomerangs. Bread cast upon the waters, I have discovered, sometimes simply sinks, and efforts to give someone a boost up the ladder often results in getting your fingers stepped on.

"Never be nice to an actor," Percy Hammond once warned. "It might bite you."

I've spent the better part of a lifetime consorting with actors, even being nice to some of them at times, and I have the fang marks to attest to the wisdom of Hammond's advice. I don't think that actors mean to be as carnivorous as they are. It's just that the pursuit of fame for a performer is as precarious as a steeplechase, and it is impossible to engage in it without getting an occasional elbow in the eye. An actor has to resort to any stratagem to get ahead in his precarious calling, and most of them will cheerfully abandon home, mother or even press agent for a meaty role, a good review or a favorable marquee billing.

I once did a special show on N.B.C., on which I also functioned as producer, so I was cast in the role of referee in the inevitable scuffle over which performers would get top billing. Shelley Berman was one of the guests scheduled to appear and I was not surprised when he suggested that the performers be listed alphabetically. However, I was surprised when Charley Weaver cheerfully agreed—since his name would put him at the bottom of the listing.

"Are you sure an alphabetical listing is okay with you?" I asked Charley, a little incredulously.

"Absolutely," Charley answered. "Of course, in this instance I'd like to be billed under my real name, Cliff Arquette."

Actors are not alone in their billing consciousness and it

remained for a group of comedy writers to challenge the deity for top billing. This occurred after Red Skelton appeared as a guest on our show one night. I complimented Red on his inventive clowning and he said that some of his wild bits just came to him while he was performing. "I guess it's the working of the Almighty," Red said.

"That burned up my writers," Skelton confessed to me afterward. "They called a protest meeting with C.B.S. and made a big thing about it. One of them asked 'Has God written anything funny for you lately?' "

I once had my own problems with a writer over the matter of billing, although it had nothing to do with vanity. Once, some years ago, Maurice Zolotow, a well-known writer, interviewed me for a three-part series in *The American Weekly*.

Maurice, a likable chap, seemed impressed, or possibly stunned, by how much I could say in one interview, and said he would like to write the story in the first person. He asked if I would mind if he billed the series as "by Jack Paar as told to Maurice Zolotow." I assured him I didn't care how it was billed. Some time went by without the series appearing and eventually I forgot all about it.

A few months later, I was approached to write my autobiography. I felt a little young for such literary folly but when large sums of money were bandied about I became strangely fascinated. My saga, it transpired, was to be serialized in *Look* magazine, condensed in the *Reader's Digest*, published as a book and later as a paperback. The money involved was well over six figures.

I expressed surprise at the amounts of money ricocheting around in our conversations, for my story had been printed so often in magazines and papers that even my mother was tired of reading it. However, the publishers pointed out that, although it was true that my story had a lot of mileage on it, this would be the first time *I* had ever told my own story, which was what made it valuable. Straight from the horse's mouth and all that sort of thing, they explained.

Suddenly a bell clanged in the back of my mind. I remembered Zolotow and our vague conversation about putting my name on the story along with his. I mentioned this to the publishers, who turned faint at the tidings.

"Do you realize that if you gave permission for your name to appear on the series you have already told your life story?" my agent groaned. "Here you're being offered a fortune for it, and it sounds as if you've already given it away."

A hasty check confirmed my ominous recollection. As I had vaguely remembered, the series was told in the first person and bore my name as well as Zolotow's. To add insult to injury, the editor who had ordered the series had left *The American Weekly*. The new editor hadn't liked it and didn't plan to run it. Not only had I given away my life story, but it was sitting on a dusty shelf instead of garnering me money, being enshrined in the Library of Congress or being buried in a time capsule.

We made cautious overtures to the magazine and they finally grudgingly agreed to sell the series back to me for what they paid Zolotow for it. So for $3,500 I was finally able to buy back my own life!

Although egos tend to sprout in all corners of show business, narcissism is particularly an occupational hazard among actors. The limelight has a tendency to swell heads as big as Matanuska Valley cabbages and to give personalities a hickory-cured flavor. Moreover, gratitude seems as rare among actors as modesty.

Because I happen to have at my disposal more than nine hours weekly of midnight television time, which sells for $11,000 a minute, I have been in the happy position of being able to assist a good many performers and it has been curious to note some of their reactions.

Most of them, of course, are genuinely grateful for the national exposure, which is so important to any performer, but a few have responded in rather odd ways. Some, being paid to entertain, blatantly sneaked in paid plugs for commercial products and a few even used the show to sound off on a personal grievance against someone, thus involving N.B.C. and me in lawsuits. One singing group badgered us for months to get on and then said, in a magazine interview, that being on was "like listening to a Methodist minister who has had four martinis."

Others swore eternal gratitude for the break, after exposure on our show had zoomed them to stardom, only to be struck dumb at a time when I could have used their moral support in my hassle with Ed Sullivan.

An example of this was a comedy team who were knocking around the country playing obscure night clubs before exposure of their fine talents on our show rocketed them into the $10,000-an-appearance class on big shows like Ed Sullivan's. Yet when Sullivan said, in effect, that performers had to choose between his show and ours, I heard no further protestations of loyalty from them.

Myron Cohen, the talented monologist, was another performer who went AWOL when Sullivan served his ultimatum. Not long before, when Cohen had been criticized for telling dialect stories, I defended him on the air, saying that he handled his stories with such good taste that no one could take offense. Cohen sent me a warm telegram expressing his thanks and saying that he was looking forward to appearing on our show in the near future.

His appearance was scheduled the night that Sullivan dropped his bombshell and Cohen was the first to cancel.

Some of the most curious reactions I have encountered have been from performers who achieved success through our program and were so grateful that they wanted to help me out. One unknown comedian, who became a top attraction after many appearances with us, began dropping around shortly afterward, giving me little tips on how to be funnier. *My* success had gone to *his* head.

Actually, I have always felt that anyone who got a break through our show did as much if not more for us than we did for him, and I have been amply rewarded by their performances and by my pleasure at whatever success they have achieved. Exposure on our show isn't automatically an open sesame to fame, however, as it has been for some especially talented people like Shelley Berman, Dody Goodman, Joey Bishop, Phyllis Diller, Peggy Cass and others. Nevertheless, throughout the life of the show I have been badgered by people who felt I had it in my power to make them a success overnight—and that if I didn't do it I was a bum.

One such was an impresario friend of mine who wrote quite a good book about his experiences in the theater. In fact, I was quite flattered to hear he had dedicated it to me until I discovered I was included in a mass dedication which seemed to outnumber the population of Duluth, Minnesota. If everyone included in the dedication had bought a copy, it would have sold more copies than *Peyton Place*.

In any event, I liked the author and when he came to me and asked if I would have him on the show to talk about the book, to spur its sales, I readily agreed. Not long afterward he called me and said that the book still wasn't surging to the top of the best seller list, and could he come on again. I put him on again, and a few more times after that. I think he was on a total of five times, plugging the book and getting $320 each time for doing it. Then I got another call from him.

"Look here," he said, rather testily. "Moss Hart's book is still number one on the best seller list. What are *we* going to do about it?"

The female of the species, in show business as in life, is often deadlier than the male, and sometimes seems to take greater relish in repaying a pat on the back with a kick in the shins. I learned this little lesson while producing my own Special for N.B.C. For the show I signed a well-known lady singer. I agreed to pay her $15,000 to sing two songs—the most she was ever paid for a single appearance up to that time, and possibly since.

In addition, the lady's manager came to me a few days before the show and said they had problems and needed the money in advance. Accordingly I paid them before, so I thought I had done rather well by the lady.

I didn't see her again until some months later when we were both scheduled to appear on the *Perry Como Show*. When I arrived at the theater for rehearsal I was told my dressing room was 301. I went there, left my hat, coat and brief case, and reported back to the stage.

I was sitting waiting for the rehearsal to begin, when the stage manager came up and said, "Would you mind if we moved you up one floor to 401? 301 is a little nicer and our guest singer asked if she could have it."

"I don't mind at all," I said. "I'll run up and move my things."

"That won't be necessary," the stage manager said. "She already moved them."

Oddly enough my only other public *contretemps* with a lady also started when I made a guest appearance on another show. I don't know how I get into these situations with the opposite sex. I bow to no man in my appreciation of girls, particularly pretty girls, and I've always tried to heed the admonition I learned at my mother's knee—never strike a lady when she's down. However, there are times when no display of masculine gallantry can keep you from becoming embroiled with some member of the tender sex.

This one started when I made a guest appearance on the *Jack Benny Show* in Hollywood. While rehearsing I met Joyce Davidson, a blond eyeful who was doing some commercials on the program. Miss Davidson, I learned, hailed from Saskatoon, Saskatchewan, and had slashed her way into television chopping onions for a home-economics show.

I suppose I should have been more cautious with someone so deft at wielding a blade, even against onions. And the deceptively peaceful-looking Miss Davidson was no stranger to controversy, having stirred up a rumpus in Canada with some remarks about Queen Elizabeth which didn't sit kindly with the Canadians.

However, she seemed like a pleasant and pretty girl and, when she asked me to tape an interview with her for a program she had on the Canadian Broadcasting Company network, I was putty in her hands. The tape was duly shown on her show in Canada and I felt I had made my little contribution to her permanent emancipation from onion-slicing.

Nearly two years later, the Westinghouse Broadcasting Company slotted a new program called *P.M. East/P.M. West* opposite our late night opus with the avowed intention of luring away our insomniac audience. Joyce Davidson, I was pleased to see, was to be one of their mainstays.

The first night I noticed they used Shelley Berman, Earl Grant, Jonathan Winters and others who appear more or less regularly on our show, which hinted, I felt, that originality was not one of the main ingredients of *P.M. East/P.M. West*. However, the new program had an even more lethal weapon to use against me. It was *me!* Miss Davidson had resurrected the old interview I had done nineteen months before for her Canadian show and blithefully announced that she was going to run it on *P.M. East* at the same time as our show.

This threat held no terrors for me. If there is one performer whose talents don't scare me it's Jack Paar. Also, I felt the charming Jack Paar of today, in vivid living color, was more than a match for the Jack Paar of nineteen months before, dredged up on Miss Davidson's old taped interview. However, N.B.C. and my agents, M.C.A., took no such philosophical view of the matter.

They began to mutter darkly about legal actions if *P.M.*

East showed the tape. At this, Miss Davidson set up a howl that could be heard all the way back to her old home town of Saskatoon. She issued a statement the tone of which would have done justice to a pronouncement from the United Nations. Freedom of speech around the world would be threatened, she claimed, if she couldn't show her dusty taped interview with me.

"Americans criticized the Soviet Union for not allowing Gromyko's U.N. appearances to be seen in Russia," she trumpeted. "How can Mr. Paar's office and M.C.A. in good conscience defend this illiberal action?"

How 'bout dot?—as my friend, José Melis, might say.

Dealing with performers is said to be a hazardous calling and having indulged in such perilous relations for years I have to admit that this is indeed true. Yet there is someone even more difficult than the most temperamental performer—a performer's wife.

One day I received a rather hysterical phone call from the wife of a young, rather far-out comedian, who had appeared on our show a couple of times. The comedian, his wife tearfully informed me, had been arrested on a narcotics charge.

She declared vehemently that the accusation against him was a bum rap, a dirty lie, an outrage, and, moreover, that it wasn't even true. I was touched by her obvious sincerity and the details she cited did make it seem that the comic was not guilty.

Caught up in his wife's vehemence, I charged into the fray. On the program I talked about the situation and said that I believed, from what I had heard on the case, that the comedian was innocent. I got rather carried away at what seemed like an injustice, and waxed pretty emotional about the whole thing.

A nationally syndicated columnist interviewed me and I defended the comedian, appealing for a careful study of the charges against him. As a result, I felt really gratified when the charges against him were dismissed in court.

Some time passed and I forgot all about the incident. Then one night, in discussing a record album of Jonathan Winters', I mentioned that he was nearly as far-out as the young comedian. I thought it was a compliment since I admire them both, including the fact that their humor has often been further out than Yuri Gagarin.

The next day I got a heated telegram from the comedian's wife. She was fit to be tied, and I wish someone *had* tied her. She said she had heard my crack about her husband and was not amused. "You are only happy when you're defending my husband by doing your crying act," she said. "If he's ever in trouble again I'll call you."

Only my natural gallantry restrained me from replying that he *is* in trouble. He's married to her.

3

The Power of Positive Drinking

I LONG AGO reconciled myself to the fact that our show would never win any citations from Alcoholics Anonymous or the Women's Christian Temperance Union. There has always been something about facing a microphone or TV camera that makes almost anyone wish for a good stiff drink, and on our show this impulse has sometimes reached epic proportions.

Charley Weaver has always been the pace setter of our little group, ever since the Christmas he came on in a Santa Claus suit, filled with Yuletide cheer, and almost got the extremely proper Mary Margaret McBride inebriated by merely sitting next to her and hiccoughing.

There was also the celebrated occasion on which Mickey Rooney came on tipsy, after celebrating his first wedding anniversary with his fifth wife. The next night Red Skelton spoke of Mickey's boozy appearance.

"I don't drink any more," Red said. "Of course," he added, "I don't drink any less either."

After having interviewed thousands of people over the years, I'm still amazed at the widely varying reactions to facing an audience. Some of the greatest stars, who have spent a lifetime in the theater, suffer from extreme jitters before going on while often a total amateur, with no experience at all, remains completely calm.

Tallulah Bankhead, a great actress and a lively, nonstop conversationalist, is one of the most nervous guests I ever had. Another is Jean Kerr, the writer, who smokes to calm her nerves. One night, while I was interviewing her, she had three cigarettes going at once.

Peggy Cass is another jittery one. Before the show Peggy paces wildly about protesting that she can't think of a thing to say. Then she comes plunging through the curtains and it's almost impossible to stop her.

Selma Diamond, the comedy writer, is now *blasé* about her air appearances, but the first time she came on she was so nervous that when she went to the ladies' room we posted sentries outside the door for fear she would try to escape.

Other guests, however, show no qualms at all. Bob Hope fairly reeks of confidence, and George Jessel would never win any prize at a flower show for shrinking violets. And Alex King needs nothing stronger than a glass of milk to talk endlessly and entertainingly without a trace of nerves.

I can understand why people some feel the need of a drink as a stiffener, although I don't indulge much in strong drink myself. This is not out of any great virtue but just that I don't seem to require artificial stimulants; I appear to have been born with an edge on. Also, liquor affects me the way it does Indians.

I swore off overindulgence in the grape after an incident some years ago in a New York restaurant. Miriam and I were having dinner with another couple, and had had a couple of martinis, when across the room I spied two gag writers I had known in Hollywood.

We had not been exactly bosom friends in the film capital, but in the roseate glow from the martinis they looked suddenly as welcome as Stanley must have appeared to Livingstone.

I fell all over them with happy cries. This ardent reunion inevitably led to a couple of more martinis and before long I had reached the state which Bishop Sheen describes as "amiable incandescence."

My memory of the later stages of the evening is a little confusing. When Miriam and our friends finally propelled me toward the door, I began to get the distinct impression that I was aboard ship and the deck was pitching badly in a storm.

As we emerged from the restaurant I suddenly felt seasick and grabbed what looked through the haze like a mast, but which actually proved to be one of the poles holding up the cafe's canopy. Although I grasped it frantically, I could feel myself sliding down the pole until my chin met the sidewalk with a muffled clunk. For the rest of what happened I have to rely on Miriam, who gave me the lurid details when she resumed speaking to me several days later.

It seems that as I made my descent down the pole face-first, my friends rushed to the rescue. Grasping me firmly under my arms, the other husband hoisted me to an upright position. However, my limp form slithered out of my overcoat leaving him holding the empty coat, while I again pitched face-down on the sidewalk. Eventually Miriam and my friends lifted me into a cab and got me home, but I have renounced strong drink in large quantities ever since.

Betty Hutton, who hardly needs any additional stimulation, once came on the show well fortified for the ordeal. As she arrived at the elevators to go up to our studio, Betty saw the line of people waiting to be taken up. For some reason, this brought out the crusader in her.

Planting herself in line with the ticket holders, she announced that she wouldn't go up unless the entire audience went too. The pages explained that the audience would be admitted to the studio at the regular time, but Betty would have none of it. With the fervor of a Joan of Arc, the blond actress declared that she was leading the downtrodden ticket holders to the sixth-floor studio. It was all or no one, she announced in fiery tones.

Shaken up by this ultimatum, the N.B.C. pages capitulated.

Triumphantly, Betty was borne to the studio, leading the liberated ticket holders.

I'm used to hearty greetings from some guests, but she flung herself at me like a playful panther. She kissed me ardently, and bussed Hugh Downs and José Melis. I feared she was going to kiss the entire orchestra but she desisted after working her way through the string section.

When she finally left, after what might loosely be termed an interview, I was afraid to strike a match for fear the studio would light up like a plum pudding.

Some people have gotten so stoned in getting ready for the show that they never made it at all. One such was a famous humorist, one of the funniest writers alive but terrified of two things—TV cameras and airplanes.

The night he was to be on my show he was not only slated to face the cameras but was also scheduled to catch a plane after the show to fly to Hollywood and appear on Groucho Marx's show.

Early in the afternoon, I began getting bulletins on his condition. He had lunch with Tom Cochran, my associate producer, to run over possible subjects to talk about, and began to brace himself for the ordeal ahead. By the time he had braced himself his nervousness was dissipated, but so were his wits.

The next bulletin I got was from a Turkish bath, where Tommy reported the author was sweating out the beers. Finally I received word that he had been done to a turn in the Turkish bath but was in no condition to appear on television. In fact, I was told, it would be quite a feat if they got him poured aboard the plane that night for Hollywood and his appearance with Groucho.

He didn't make *that*, either!

I later learned that when he did fly to Hollywood he was higher than the plane. Once on solid ground again, he felt the urgent need of an eye-opener to maintain his newly found courage and repaired to the Brown Derby bar. There he fueled his courage up to new heights, when Groucho happened to walk into the restaurant.

Feeling no shyness at all by this time, the writer greeted Groucho effusively and informed him he was prepared to be at his most scintillating on the comedian's show that night. Noting the author's condition, Groucho showed no great enthusiasm at this announcement.

This wounded the writer to the quick. He stood up and denounced Groucho roundly before the startled restaurant patrons. He told him what he could do with his TV show and, as an afterthought, added he could do the same thing with the N.B.C. transmitter. With that he stalked out and flew back to New York.

He is probably the only man who ever flew six thousand miles just *not* to be on two television shows.

Although many guests have come on our show in various stages of intoxication, only one that I know of went out and got drunk as a *result* of being on. That was Brendan Behan, the rumpled Irish playwright who is almost as renowned a tosspot as he is a writer.

Behan first attracted attention for his heroic drinking exploits in London, where his play, *The Hostage,* was showing. On several occasions, after indulging too freely in what he calls "the gargle," Behan showed up at the theater in London's West End and heckled the actors, wrangled with the audience and broke into song.

Despite his fondness for drink, Behan is a talented writer and witty conversationalist. "Brendan has a great message," actor Michael MacLiammoir once remarked, "if he doesn't spill it."

Brendan had a rough upbringing and was jailed by the British for pro-Irish activities. He later was accused of being left wing. "I did help collect food for Republican Spain in the Spanish Civil War," he admitted. "But the depression was on and we ate most of it ourselves."

Behan is a colorful but nonstop conversationalist. "The only time Brendan pauses when he's talking," Alex King said, "is to sing. Trying to talk with him is like a butterfly going through a meat grinder."

Edwin O'Connor, the author, once had lunch with Behan at the fashionable Ritz hotel in Boston. Behan was his boisterous, genial self, laughing, talking and joking in a loud voice. An elderly and dignified Boston Brahmin entered the room, took one look at the noisy Irishman and fled.

"*That*," he said as he departed, "is the kind of person who voted for Kennedy."

Before I met him, I had heard stories of how fast Behan was on the comeback. While he was working on *The Hostage*, a reporter called and asked for his comment on an Irish statesman's speech attacking Irish writers who hold Ireland up to ridicule.

"I can't comment on that," said Behan. "I'm too busy writing a play holding the Irish up to ridicule."

Another time an interviewer asked, "What would you like said of yourself fifty years from today?"

"That I'm eighty-seven years old," answered the 37-year-old writer.

Despite his reputation, Behan was the soul of decorum the first night he came on our show. "I'm off the gargle for good," he assured me. "Not just for Lent. For breadth as well."

But even stone sober, the Irish playwright turned out to be a man of provocative opinions. "Occasionally there's a day-cent raymark made on the telly," he said. "But this is only occasionally."

We discussed drinking and I commented on the virtues of temperance. Brendan complained that his trouble is that he looks drunk even when he is sober—a point that I had to concede. He has wild hair, a broken nose, a torso that seems to be terraced and his teeth, several of which are missing, look like milestones along a winding country road.

While we spoke of the evils of drink, I mentioned the advice given me by Leo Genn, the actor. "If it has to be women or drink, take women," he counseled me, "because drink always leads to women but women don't necessarily lead to drink."

At one point in the conversation, Geneviève was prompted to extol the virtues of French champagne. Behan, who has lived in France, agreed that champagne was a fine drink. I thought I detected a nostalgic look in his eye as Geneviève rattled on about the joys of drinking "shom-pine."

After the show, Brendan and his wife got into a tiff backstage. Afterward he apparently decided to drown his anger in some of the champagne that Geneviève had talked so enthusiastically about. At any rate he fell spectacularly off the wagon.

The next night he came wobbling down the aisle of the theater, shortly after the second act of his play began, and interrupted the performance. "I've brought you the finest actors and actresses in the world—and a good play," he shouted. "If you don't believe me, I don't give a damn."

Then he hoisted himself onto the stage, where he did a jig and sang, "It's an old Irish tune . . . I'll be there soon."

That was only the beginning. His fall off the wagon that began after our show turned into a monumental coast-to-coast bender. In New York, he got banned from the St. Patrick's Day Parade. In San Francisco, he tried to jump into the Bay. In Hollywood, he got arrested for fighting with a policeman. He was also arrested in Toronto for brawling.

The fight broke out when he took exception to the remarks of a Canadian who was belittling U.S. space achievements. Behan bellowed, "My friend, Ireland will put a shillalah into orbit, Israel will put a matzoh ball into orbit, and Liechtenstein will put a postage stamp into orbit before you Canadians ever put up as much as a mouse."

"Do you know," Behan mused later, "he hit me just for that?"

After my experience with Behan, I swore off giving temperance lectures. My one to him seemed to have driven him to drink.

4

Stocks on the Rocks

I ALWAYS WANTED to write a "how to" book, but most of the things that have happened to me seem to illustrate how not to.

One day, while perusing the best seller lists, to ponder the latest position of my book, *I Kid You Not,* I discovered that a Hungarian dancer named Nicolas Darvas, of the team of Darvas and Julia, had written a best seller titled *How I Made Two Million Dollars in the Stock Market.*

Since all you could do by buying my own book was lose $3.95, I rushed out to buy Darvas' and plunged avidly into it. Like a lot of other people, I suppose, I figured that if someone who dances the Tango for a living could make two million dollars playing the market, maybe even I could.

The book made it all sound so easy. Here, while the rest of us had been beating our brains out to make a living, Nick Darvas had been grandly touring the world, doing a few turns with the beautiful Julia and, in the process, calmly making a fortune on the stock market by remote control.

The way he got started, Darvas explained, was when a nightclub owner, who couldn't afford to pay him, gave him some bum stock instead, so the dancer made a fortune in self defense.

If Darvas could make two million dollars while doing the Cha Cha Cha with Julia, why couldn't I get rich the same way, while exchanging small talk with Geneviève and Betty White?

After all, I had dabbled a bit in the market. I once took a little flier in a tapioca mine. And another time, on a tip from

Jack Douglas, I invested in a chain of wishing wells he was starting.

But now I wanted to get into the market in a big way. Not content with practically memorizing Darvas' book, I corralled him in the flesh and pumped him for details. I got the whole story, straight from the horse's mouth.

Armed with this, I began playing the market. Suddenly I acquired a whole corps of volunteer advisers. It seemed as though everyone in show business was suddenly playing the market, and most of them had advice for me. Even George Jessel, who has a perfect record. He's never picked a winner yet.

Georgie was once called by a Congressional probe because of his investments in cotton futures. On that occasion he assured the Congressmen, "There are three things I will never try again: (1) embracing an ostrich; (2) marrying a certain lady; and (3) investing in cotton futures."

But even though Jessel had retired from the investment field, he was full of words of wisdom. He also introduced me to some of his rich friends. Soon I was getting tips from millionaires—men who actually owned big companies—not necessarily a foolproof way of beating the market, as I discovered and as Groucho Marx later told me.

Groucho related to me his own experience in losing his shirt during the crash of 1929. The day Wall Street "laid an egg," as *Variety* put it, Groucho rushed in panic to his lawyer with a list of his investments. The lawyer groaned as he studied Groucho's stocks.

"Who recommended this?" the lawyer asked, pointing to one dog.

"Bernard Baruch," answered the dazed Groucho.

"What about this one?" asked the lawyer, indicating another that had nose-dived.

"The president of General Electric," muttered Groucho.

At last the lawyer came to the one stock that hadn't tumbled.

"Who advised you on *this* one?"

"Oh, *that*," said Groucho. "A wardrobe woman at the Shubert Theater in Chicago."

Groucho told me this only after my own plunge into the market, when I thought that any tip from a tycoon was as good as money in the bank. Armed with a half-dozen such tips from high places I felt there was no way I could miss getting rich.

One of the stocks I bought was that of a gefultefish company. I had got a hot tip from a friend that it was going to merge with a big soap company, and the stock was bound to go up. Well, the gefultefish company merged, all right, but not with a soap company. It joined with, of all things, a *brassiere* company, which indicated that someone had a pretty wild sense of packaging. It was the only stock on the market that went up and *out*. And then down.

I told this story on the air, thinking it was funny, and the first thing I knew I had the Securities and Exchange Commission breathing down my neck. They summoned me to their office and wanted to know if I was up to any hanky-panky in mentioning the strange merger of the gefultefish and brassiere companies. I quickly pointed out that my only connection with the stock had been to lose money on it.

"The only way I have ever manipulated the stock market was to sell," I remarked, ruefully. "Whenever I sell a stock it immediately goes up."

Apparently the S.E.C. examiners could plainly see that I was no potential wolf of Wall Street, and dropped the matter.

My stocks kept dropping. The first thing I knew, acting on fool-proof tips, I had lost $47,000. With the tax bracket I'm in, $47,000 represented more than a year's work, but it hadn't taken me nearly that long to lose it.

I was still licking my wounds when Lou Holtz, the veteran comedian, appeared as a guest on our show. Lou is reputedly one of the shrewdest investors in show business, and admits, cheerfully, to having made three million dollars on stocks.

Everything Lou touches turns to money, even if it's only a mashie. When he joined the Hillcrest Country Club in Los Angeles, they struck oil. He gets a check for sixty-one dollars every month from his share.

I mentioned that I had lost $47,000 on the market in a few months and Lou seemed touched by my stock-market *naïveté*. He said he would give me a tip on a stock then selling for ten dollars a share that in ten years would be selling for a thousand dollars.

Still wary after my scrape with the S.E.C., I cautioned him not to mention the name of the stock on the air.

"I wouldn't think of it," he said. "We'd all get arrested."

Lou didn't mention the name of the stock, but even his hint was enough to start a national commotion. While we were still on the air, the N.B.C. switchboard lit up with hundreds of callers from all over the country. Everyone wanted to know the name of the stock. I had to change my unlisted phone number and Lou went underground.

The effect on the stock market was immediate. Even though Holtz had not mentioned the stock by name, he had said it was selling around ten dollars, so thousands of people began second-guessing.

There were about twenty-five stocks selling at around ten dollars at that time, but rumors concentrated on two of them, with spectacular results. One, M.P.O. Videotronics, had been trading a few hundred shares. Its volume increased to 61,000 overnight and it quickly jumped from 10 to 15¾.

The stock that Holtz had actually been talking about— Canadian Javelin—also climbed quickly. Its volume rose from 4,400 to 71,900 overnight, and it went from 9½, the day of the TV tip, to 12¼ the next day.

Meantime, the phone at my N.B.C. office was jumping off the hook as friends, and friends of friends, and friends of enemies all called to ask the name of the stock. One call was from my old friends at the S.E.C.

The S.E.C. man said sternly, "We'd like you to come down to our office."

"I don't want to see you," I replied. "You're the ones who want to see me. So why don't *you* come to *my* office?"

Somewhat to my surprise, they showed up the next day. Two very pleasant S.E.C. men dropped in and asked for full details about the stock-market flurry. It was a little hard to talk, because the phone kept ringing as more people called to ask the name of the stock, but I explained the whole incident as best I could.

"The way I figure it is that Holtz deliberately planned the whole thing," I said. "I think he has telephone stock."

On this light-hearted suggestion, the S.E.C. men departed, apparently satisfied that the law had not been broken.

The S.E.C. also summoned Holtz. "What have you to say about all this?" they asked him.

"All I have to say," said Lou, seriously, "is buy the stock."

5

Laughter on the New Frontier

I DON'T KNOW MUCH about politics—except that it seems to be the only field besides show business where everyone is an expert—but there's one thing I like about President Kennedy's New Frontier. Mr. Kennedy has a sense of humor.

I suppose a sharp wit isn't a prime requisite for the highest office in the land, but, other things being equal, it is a wonderful asset, as the warm humor of Abraham Lincoln has shown.

Not since the days of Lincoln, alas, has a President been really noted for his wit or appreciation of humor. In fact, until lately a sense of humor has been looked on as something of a liability in a President. This may be due to the fact that Adlai Stevenson, an inveterate and polished quipster, was twice roundly trounced by Dwight Eisenhower who projected the stern, no-nonsense air of his military background.

Most of our Presidents have been serious men and some of them seem to have considered smiling a violation of their oath of office. Calvin Coolidge, a taciturn Vermonter, was as glum as Ed Sullivan. Herbert Hoover was a fine President, but he never smiled much either. Maybe it was those tight collars.

Harry Truman once did an impersonation of H. V. Kaltenborn, and even went on TV with Jack Benny, but his humor —well, maybe I'd better not comment on that. Mr. Truman is easily aroused by detractors, and *I* don't want to get one of those letters from him.

Of all the recent Presidents, I suppose that Franklin D. Roosevelt had the best sense of humor. He had a buoyant personality, was an instructive actor, and people who knew him tell me he was a zestful *raconteur*. But from what I've read of the give-and-take of his press conferences, he was less effective at ad-lib banter.

Mr. Kennedy's sense of humor first manifested itself publicly long before he ran for the Presidency. In fact, it came to light in the first public speech he ever made—as a young lieutenant in Naval Intelligence early in World War II. He had been assigned to address groups of factory workers in South Carolina on the differences between two types of incendiary bombs, and he acquitted himself very well. However, flushed with success, he pushed his luck a little too far.

After finishing his speech he asked, "Are there any questions?"

A man in the audience got up and asked the inexperienced new lieutenant a long, rambling and highly technical question.

"I'm glad you asked that," Kennedy grinned. "We have a man coming to talk to you in a few weeks who may be able to answer it."

Mr. Kennedy's sense of humor showed itself early in the campaign. On one occasion his campaign train pulled out unexpectedly just as he had finished a speech from the rear platform. Several startled newsmen were left standing on the station platform as the train disappeared down the tracks.

Waving cheerfully at the stranded reporters, Kennedy yelled, "Be sure to write!"

Throughout the campaign, Senator Kennedy was subjected to considerable Republican twitting about his wealth. He invariably turned away these jibes gracefully and with humor.

Once, when charged with lavish spending on his behalf by his family, Kennedy made light of the charges by reading this supposed wire from his father: "Jack, don't buy a single vote more than is necessary. I'll be damned if I'm going to pay for a landslide."

Later, Kennedy worried Democratic fund-raisers when he

announced that if elected he didn't intend handing out important ambassadorships to anyone just because he had been a big contributor to the party.

"Ever since I made that announcement," he cracked later at a banquet, "I have not received one cent from my father."

I first met President Kennedy through his younger brother, Robert, and I met Bobby the way I meet so many people— we shared a lawsuit together.

Before the 1960 conventions, Bobby Kennedy had come on my show to discuss his book dealing with labor-management racketeering. He made such an attractive, outspoken and articulate guest, and his appearance made such an impact on the public, that there were some dark mutterings about my allowing the program to be used as an electioneering forum by the Kennedys.

There was even talk that Bobby might make a better candidate than his older brother and a West Coast lawyer actually wrote to Senator Kennedy suggesting that he resign from the Senate so that his brother Robert could replace him and then run for the Presidency.

Jack Kennedy wrote to the lawyer: "This is to acknowledge your letter and to tell you that I am taking your recommendation under advisement. I have consulted Bobby about it, and, to my dismay, your idea appealed to him."

Although Bobby Kennedy made a striking impression on the show, the enthusiastic reaction to his appearance was not shared by Jimmy Hoffa, the Teamster Union president, whom Kennedy had characterized in terms not altogether favorable to Hoffa. The union chief promptly struck back by slapping a suit for $2,500,000 against Bobby, N.B.C. and me.

When a process server arrived at my office in Radio City to serve a summons on me he encountered a secretary who was new on her job but apparently had heard of my penchant for getting into legal difficulties.

Asking the process server to wait, she called my private

secretary and asked politely, "What time does Mr. Paar accept summonses?"

Not long afterward, Robert Kennedy was appointed Attorney General—the highest law enforcement office in the land.

Because of having a large chunk of midnight air at my disposal, I tried to remain strictly neutral in the election. I feel I succeeded, since the mail I got denouncing me as obviously pro-Kennedy was balanced almost exactly by the choleric correspondence I received claiming that I was clearly pro-Nixon. Actually, I felt neutral because I liked and respected both candidates.

If I had a real rooting interest in either candidate I suppose it should have been for Mr. Kennedy, since he was, in a sense, a home-town boy, having been raised in Bronxville, where I live, during the time his father, former Ambassador Joseph P. Kennedy, was in the movie business.

I was reminded of Mr. Kennedy's brief former association with our little village the day after the election when our local paper carried the headline:

FORMER BRONXVILLE MAN ELECTED PRESIDENT

Another amusing example of this kind of charming insularity occurred shortly afterward when the President-Elect's wife presented him with a baby son. *Variety*, the "bible of show business," heralded the news:

> Mr. and Mrs. John F. Kennedy, Nov. 25,
> Washington, a son, John F. Kennedy, Jr.
> Child is grandson of Joseph P. Kennedy,
> former President of Film Booking Office
> and R.K.O. Theatres.

After Jack Kennedy's election as President, I had the honor of being invited to the Inauguration, an event which was labelled "Nixon's Revenge" because of the blizzard which turned the festivities into what could have passed for a revival of *Nanook of the North*.

Although actors have understandably been viewed with some suspicion in the capital, ever since John Wilkes Booth's unfortunate performance during "Our American Cousin" at Ford's Theater, Washington was crowded with performers who entertained at the Gala. They didn't get paid for the Gala performance, Joey Bishop told me, but Peter Lawford, the actor who is the President's brother-in-law, had arranged for them each to pose for a stamp.

In addition to the horde of actors, Washington was crawling with Kennedys, former Harvard professors and touch-football players—and I use the word crawling advisedly. The blizzard had snarled traffic, and most people, including Miriam and I, got where we were going by wading through the snow.

Miriam looked beautiful in her Inauguration gown, and I had reluctantly consented to be trussed up in tails, but long woolen underwear would have been more appropriate. In my formal clothes, and the freezing weather, I not only looked but felt like a penguin.

We finally made it to the Gala and the Inaugural Ball, but only after mushing through the snow for blocks. Poor Geneviève, who was so proud of her lovely new gown, arrived in borrowed Army boots looking like *Tess of the Storm Country*.

The Ball was a shambles and if Cinderella had been there I'm sure she'd have fled by nine-thirty. The ballroom was so jammed that dancing was as rugged as ice hockey, and the floor was so slippery from spilled drinks I thought of asking the orchestra to play the "Skater's Waltz."

Even amid all this chaos, however, the President's sense of humor didn't desert him. Looking around at the sea of bedraggled dancers, he said wryly, "I think this is the ideal way to spend an evening. I suggest we meet here again, same time, same place, tomorrow night."

Despite the snow and the resultant rugged conditions, there

are many wonderful memories of the big day—the President's stirring Inaugural Address; wonderful old Robert Frost reciting his poem, which he couldn't see and I couldn't understand; the lectern beginning to smoke as Cardinal Cushing was giving the Invocation.

As I noticed the smoke, from an electrical short-circuit, start enveloping the praying Cardinal, I whispered in alarm, "What's that?"

"Holy smoke," Miriam answered.

During our stay in Washington, it was impossible not to be struck by the fresh vigor that the new young President had brought to the capital. Mr. Kennedy, and his lovely wife Jacqueline, seemed to thrive on the march to the New Frontier, although it left most of the rest of us footsore and puffing.

The President not only bounced buoyantly from one official affair to another, but managed to drop in unexpectedly a couple of times on old friends, without seemingly ever running out of steam. On the night of the Gala I got a chance to talk with the new President at a private party which his father gave for some of their friends afterward. The party was a pleasant one, and I thoroughly enjoyed it, although I did get a bit of a start when I saw the serious-looking Senator Mc-Clellan of Arkansas, whom I had last seen on television sternly grilling labor racketeers, doing rather an abandoned Cha Cha Cha.

President Kennedy is extremely informal, and has great charm, but I was taken aback by the Hollywood-type familiarity with which some of the show people present talked to him. Several of them would be well qualified if the President ever creates the post of Secretary of Offense.

I shuddered when I heard Milton Berle say to the chief executive, "You're a nice fella, Jack, but I don't think you're handling your career right."

However, the President accepted the champagne-charged familiarity with good humor and without losing dignity. He was put to the ultimate test, in this respect, while talking with me, when a noisy gent who had obviously taken aboard too much anti-freeze as a precaution against the cold came up and buttonholed Mr. Kennedy with a boisterousness usually seen only at class reunions or American Legion conventions. The President politely but deftly untangled himself from the octopus-like grasp of his effusive admirer and slipped away, leaving the tipsy bore talking to someone else. Me!

I got another demonstration of the boundless Kennedy energy when we were invited to lunch by Bobby and Ethel Kennedy at Hickory Hill, their charming, 140-year-old home in the rolling hills near McLean, Virginia.

We were greeted at the door by Ethel, who had just come in from skiing with her tribe of children, after having danced until the wee hours the night before. Sure enough, the first thing I spotted as we entered their foyer was a soggy football.

There were a number of Hollywood stars present, and the luncheon was conducted in an informal atmosphere of charming bedlam. While cocktails were being served, the front door flew open and in bounded a panting Irish setter. Moments later another setter loped in, closely followed by a large damp St. Bernard, who plopped down in the middle of the room. Then came a whoop and four of the seven Kennedy children came sliding down the bannister to join the hubbub.

Later the doorbell rang and in trooped at least a full team of Harvard football players. Thereafter, cocktails and luncheon were served by waiters who had to exercise great care not to step on the kids, dogs or scattered athletic equipment. At one point, a plate of food fell on the floor and one of the dogs swiftly gobbled it up, except for a few leaves of lettuce.

"He *never* eats lettuce," Ethel shrugged.

I chatted with the bright, freckle-faced Kennedy youngsters and heard about their awesome collection of pets. Bobby, Jr., who seemed to be the chief zoo keeper, said they had frogs, lizards, cats, dogs, birds, chickens, geese and horses.

"We had a seal," another volunteered, "but we had to give him to the zoo. We had a skunk, too, but he got lost."

While chatting with the children, I also made the acquaintance of the little Kennedy girl about whom Bobby Kennedy had told me a story. During the hearings of the McClellan Committee, which were televised, he arrived home one night filled with a sense of accomplishment over his strenuous tussles with the balky union witnesses.

"Well, honey," he asked his daughter, "how did you think the hearings went?"

"You were fine, Daddy," she said, "but the hearings ran fifteen minutes into Mickey Mouse!"

At that lunch I also talked with Bobby about the opposition to his appointment as Attorney General because of his youth and the fact that his legal experience had been confined to acting as counsel for senatorial committees. He had never actually tried a case in court. Laughing, he told me that the President had answered critics of his appointment by cracking, "I see no harm in letting Bobby get a little legal experience before he starts to practice law."

Between playing with his children, ministering to his guests and reminiscing with former Harvard football players, Bobby told me a story about the victorious campaign he had masterminded for his brother.

In one city, during the height of the campaign, Jack Kennedy was bowing and waving to the crowd as he was driven along in a parade in his honor. At one point, however, his driver made a wrong turn. He quickly circled the block, to get back into the parade, but found his way blocked by a stubborn cop.

"But this is Senator Jack Kennedy," the chauffeur protested. "The parade is for him."

"I don't care if he's Jack Paar," the policeman replied, firmly. "You're not goin' through here."

While the party was still going strong I noticed that Bobby and Ethel had disappeared. A few minutes later they reappeared. Ethel, who had been barefooted and wearing Capri pants, had slipped into a dress. Bobby had put on a dark suit and combed his tousled hair.

"Where are you going?" I asked, surprised, as they headed for the door.

"I have to go into Washington," Bobby grinned, "and get sworn in as Attorney General."

I never dreamed, as a young radio announcer in Cleveland, where I got arrested for not returning a library book, that one day I would know the highest law enforcement officer in the world. I think Bobby Kennedy is making a great Attorney General and I wouldn't be surprised if someday he became President.

6

How to Stand Up to Khrushchev, in One Easy Lesson

"THIS IS the first time in the long history of the American Union when two men have run for the Presidency on *The Jack Paar Show*," grumbled political pundit James (Scotty) Reston of *The New York Times* during the 1960 campaign. "Until recently there was only one popular test—between Kennedy and Nixon," Reston added, "and now there are two. Who can stand up to Nikita Khrushchev. And who can sit down with Jack Paar."

Although I don't admire Mr. Khrushchev's politics, I was flattered to be equated with him, even tongue in cheek, as a yardstick of Presidential fitness. Because standing up to Khrushchev may not be as far removed as Mr. Reston thinks from sitting down with me. After all, we both do comedy, although I am admittedly not as versatile at it as the Soviet Premier.

Although he looks like everybody's cutup uncle, who gets a snootful and puts on lamp shades at parties, Nikita is actually quite an accomplished entertainer. He is a quick man with an ad lib and, if he wore glasses, might be sort of a Communist Jack E. Leonard. He is clever at improvising and at one rowdy U.N. session he introduced the biggest innovation in the old soft shoe since Pat Rooney—he took off one of his shoes and thumped the desk with it. Lately he has graduated to thumping the bongo drums at diplomatic receptions, and even cavorting around in elephantine fashion in Russian folk dances.

46

If this trend continues, he may revise Soviet policy to— Today the world, tomorrow the *Ed Sullivan Show!*

So it didn't seem amiss that the two candidates might visit a comedy show, particularly one as unpredictable as ours, to get a little of the feel of things. Anyone who stood up under the bombardment of commercials on our show would certainly be conditioned against the toughest Communist threats.

I was pleased when both John F. Kennedy and Richard Nixon appeared as guests on our show during the campaign and I feel that their appearances served a useful purpose. Although some staunch guardians of the public weal, like Dorothy Kilgallen, took a dim view of the candidates appearing amid flying jokes and singing commercials, their appearance under such informal circumstances revealed their human side and, in my opinion, aided voters in making an over-all evaluation of which would make the better President.

Both Mr. Kennedy and Mr. Nixon were ideal TV guests— well informed, articulate, attractive and amusing. However, I was surprised at how different each of them seemed from the public image they project. Mr. Kennedy, who had seemed boyish and lighthearted on TV and in newspaper pictures, in person was businesslike and serious. Mr. Nixon, on the other hand, who had seemed from his TV appearances to be somewhat aloof, even stern, was much more warm and pleasant than I had expected.

When the then Senator Kennedy came on, I cautioned him at the outset that I planned to ask him some tough questions.

"What do you want to ask me—if I'm a Republican or Democrat?" he asked.

Throughout the interview, Mr. Kennedy showed not only wide-ranging knowledge, but a sharp wit. He told of his campaigning and added, "Out West they made me an honorary Indian. Now I no longer cheer for our side on television westerns."

While interviewing the future President I had to wrestle with the problem of talking about global crises between commercials for face cream and lemon juice. At one point when Mr. Kennedy was discussing our country's role in the world, I got the signal it was time for another commercial.

"Forgive me," I sighed, "but before I ask you how we can save our country, first a word from our sponsor."

Later in the campaign when I interviewed Vice President Nixon, I found him an equally pleasant guest with more humor than I had thought he would have. I offered to cancel our commercials the night of his interview, but he said, graciously, "No, that's how you make your living."

Mr. Nixon was friendly and at ease during our talk, although he said smilingly that he was bothered by my first name. "Your name is Jack," he cracked. "That's a little embarrassing for me at the moment."

I asked the Vice President what he thought about the prospects of tax deduction. He said he didn't foresee any such possibility, and added with a grin, "We're still going to get the main part of your income."

At one point in the interview I stumbled across what became a big front page story. I have a habit, like many performers, when someone interrupts me, of putting my hand on the other person's arm or knee as a signal to let me finish my point. At one stage in my interview with Mr. Nixon he started to answer a question before I had quite finished asking it.

Instinctively, I put my hand on his knee, and noticed he winced. I asked him why and he disclosed, for the first time, that he had banged his knee painfully in a car door.

I asked Mr. Nixon if he ever discussed politics with his two daughters. He said that he felt, as a general rule, that children are a little young for such discussions. However, he said that his younger daughter, Julie, who was twelve, came rushing to him a few days before saying, "Come quick, Daddy, they're saying terrible things about you on television!"

Later he told me how he explained to her that criticizing people was part of politics. He told her that he was running for President and that if enough people liked him he would be elected. If not, someone else would be elected.

The twelve-year-old girl thought that over for a moment and then asked, "Who?"

"Senator Kennedy," the Vice President said.

"Senator Kennedy?" Julie exclaimed. "Oh, ho! There goes the country!"

When the conversation shifted to the Nixon children, I asked Mrs. Nixon, who was in the audience, to join us. She brought along our daughter Randy, who was sitting with her. It was a great moment for Randy but I noticed immediately that she had forgotten something.

Before Randy flew to Washington with me, Miriam had dressed her with great care in a pretty print dress and white gloves. She reminded us both that Randy should be sure to wear her white gloves when she met the Vice President. This had slipped my mind until I invited Mrs. Nixon to join us, and I noticed that Randy didn't have her gloves on. I frowned at her and glanced pointedly at her hands, but she airily ignored me.

"Your mother told you to be sure to be a lady and wear your white gloves," I chided her after the interview, "and you forgot them."

"I didn't forget them, Poppa," she protested. "I saw Mrs. Nixon wasn't wearing any and I didn't want to embarrass her."

When Richard Nixon failed to win the Presidency, in one of the closest elections in history, I often thought of what a crushing blow it must have been. How, I wondered, does a man react to losing such an important race by an eyelash? My speculation was answered in a letter from my friend Jim Bishop, written just after he had seen Mr. Nixon at Key Biscayne, Florida, shortly after the election.

This was Jim's letter:

Dear Jack:

I've been here a month at the Key Biscayne Hotel and I expect to stay all winter. Why be cold and miserable in New York when one can be warm and miserable here? Even the palm trees are crooked, but I'm not complaining and neither is Richard Nixon. He left here a bigger man than ever.

Defeat sometimes does more for a man than victory. Richard Nixon is a bigger man now than before. I met him at the Key Colony golf course and we chatted awhile at the first tee. He kept swinging a wood at blades of grass and grinning as though he had won the election. I asked him what was the most difficult thing about losing. He was most explicit.

He said that after he had conceded that the trend seemed to be in Senator Kennedy's favor, he went back to his hotel suite and he and Mrs. Nixon sat alone in a little bedroom. The children had been put to bed early. Now, in the gloom of the pre-dawn hours, they sat in silence.

There was practically no conversation, he said. There were no crowds, no sirens, no cheers, no handshaking, no brass bands, no parades—just silence. For eight years they had struggled up toward this day, and now the ashes of disappointment were dry in their mouths.

He asked her to get some rest and she said she wasn't tired. It was six A.M. when the silence was broken. Little Julie, age twelve, had awakened and popped up in bed. She ran from her room through the sitting room to her parents' room. She looked at her mother with shiny happy eyes and then at her father.

"Well," she said, bouncing up and down on her toes, "how did the election come out?"

The Vice President stopped swinging the golf club. He looked up at the blue Miami sky and his smile faded. "You want to know the most difficult moment?" he said.

"That was it. I just didn't know how to tell that happy expectant face that I had lost."

Richard Nixon, next to President Kennedy, is now the biggest man in the country. As he teed off, I said to a friend: "I'd hate to see him lose this match by a stroke."

Come on down.

JIM BISHOP

7

The Candidate Had a Good Point There

TELEVISION has its faults, heaven knows, of which I'm probably one, but it still manages to do an occasional good turn for the country. I was a party to one such good turn as the party of the second part, so to speak, when I unwittingly assisted in bringing about a suspension of the Federal Communications Commission law granting equal time to Presidential candidates during the 1960 campaign.

Actually, the equal time law was a good one in intent, aimed at not letting any legitimate candidate for major political office get more free air time than his opponents. However, it reached a point of absurdity when applied to campaigns for every office down to coroner, and when a whole gaggle of splinter parties began to get into the act with raucous cries to be heard on the public airways.

In no time, the F.C.C. was being bombarded by requests for time from such obscure groups as the New Party, the Mississippi Black and Tan Grand Old Party, the Christian National Party and the Vegetarian Party, whose slogan is "Our Steak Is in the Future."

In Texas, several candidates in a Congressional primary demanded equal time because one candidate was a weatherman on a local station. To even things up, the community might suddenly have found itself with a half dozen candidates, disguised as weathermen, all spouting the latest on "high pressure areas" and "light variable winds."

Typically, I got mixed up in the equal time question more or less by accident. One of the more hardy perennial splinter

52

candidates in the country is an eccentric Chicagoan named Lar Daly.

Daly, who campaigns in an Uncle Sam costume, complete with whiskers, has been stumping for years as the America First Party's candidate for president. Chicago, which has been able to accept Al Capone and even the Chicago Cubs without batting an eye, has seemed to accept Daly with tolerance and even amusement.

During the 1960 Presidential campaign, Senator John Kennedy and Vice President Richard Nixon both appeared as guests on my show. Senator Kennedy appeared first and when Lar Daly heard of his appearance he promptly demanded equal time. To me, this was the funniest thing to come out of Chicago since *Kukla, Fran and Ollie*.

However, Daly wasn't kidding. Moreover, the F.C.C. decreed that, under the law, the lanky Chicagoan in the Yankee Doodle getup was entitled to his equal time.

Well, Mr. Daly showed up to claim his rights, and it was quite a night. He wore his Uncle Sam suit and had a scraggly white beard that might have adorned a goat. He also wore a grim expression which left no doubt that he was not happy with the state of the world.

I explained to the audience that giving Mr. Daly equal time was the F.C.C.'s idea—not mine. This introduction did not faze the "tireless candidate." Although I tried, in fairness, to interview him on his views, as I had Senator Kennedy, he insisted on turning the interview into a harangue.

"Your only choice is America First—or death," he intoned. "I say shoot first if necessary."

The audience, which originally seemed to think that the candidate in the Uncle Sam suit was part of a comedy sketch, began to catch on that he was in dead earnest. They began to boo and hiss his wild proposals for dealing with other countries.

Daly blasted Red China for holding some American captives

and suggested that in dealing with them we drop an atom bomb first and argue afterward.

"But if we did that," Alex King broke in, "wouldn't our American captives be killed along with the Chinese?"

"They'd be better off dead," said Daly, "than living the way they are."

"I'd like to get their opinion on that," Alex snapped.

I have never heard such wild proposals as Daly put forth. If nothing else, he achieved one historical TV first—he left me speechless. On and on he droned, hammering home what he called his "Three point program."

Finally someone in the audience yelled, "If he'd take off his hat we could see his fourth point."

Daly's appearance on the program, ridiculous as it was, served a good purpose. For millions of Americans it dramatized vividly the flaw in the F.C.C. law granting equal time to all candidates. A blizzard of mail hit the F.C.C. and Capitol Hill. Congress wasted no time in passing a resolution suspending the equal-time provision for the 1960 campaign, and President Eisenhower hastily signed it.

Then I was able to give Vice President Nixon equal time to answer Lar Daly.

One of the most engaging men I have met in public life is Senator Barry Goldwater of Arizona. Politics aside, the conservative Senator is vigorous, articulate and so handsome that Senator Hubert Humphrey has suggested he should be a movie star "for 18th Century-Fox."

Senator Goldwater came on our program to oppose the Tractors-for-Freedom plan to trade Premier Castro 500 tractors in return for the release of 1,214 Cubans captured in the ill-fated invasion at the Bay of Pigs.

I was in favor of the plan, feeling that since we had sponsored the invasion, we were morally indebted to the captives. However, to fairly present both sides of the controversial issue, I invited Senator Goldwater to present the viewpoint of those opposed to the plan. He presented his views logically and forcefully and made a striking impression.

Afterward the Senator wrote an interesting column on his appearance on the program, using something I had said to draw a political analogy. He mentioned that I had said that after owning a variety of sports cars over the years, I still derived the most pleasure from the first one—a little red MG—because I had to wait and save to get it.

"It seems to me that Mr. Paar was testifying to the validity of one of the basic contentions of the conservative viewpoint," the Senator wrote in his syndicated column. "When the rich man buys an expensive plaything it has little significance because it was so easily come by. Things which come to us easily have no significance. The satisfaction we get in life comes when we do something which is difficult; when there is sacrifice involved."

The Senator has a point there. I did enjoy that little MG more than the more expensive Aston Martin, Jaguar, Thunderbird and Mercedes-Benz that I had later. However, I have a confession to make to Senator Goldwater.

One of the things I used that little MG for—in the days in Hollywood when I couldn't get a job—was to drive down to the Unemployment Office to get my check.

8

Much Ado About Dough

ON THE NIGHT of March 14, 1961, in Miami, Florida, heavy-weight champion Floyd Patterson successfully retained his title in a rousing brawl with Ingemar Johansson, the dimple-chinned Swede who trained by doing the Mambo with his shapely *fiancée*. That same night I found myself embroiled in an equally widely publicized verbal donnybrook with Ed Sullivan, the great stone face of television.

Who but I, I pondered as I read the headlined accounts of our hostilities, would find himself in a fight with an Irishman named Sullivan on the eve of St. Patrick's Day?

Actually it was easy. As is usual with me, I didn't fall into trouble—I was pushed. Although the newspapers made a great hullabaloo about our dispute, I never considered it very earth-shaking. In fact, I didn't even plan to mention it in this book. But there was an important principle involved, and one on which I have strong opinions. I am recounting what actually happened here, as the issue could come up again.

The surprising thing about finding myself at odds with Sullivan was that I had always liked him and considered him something of a national institution—like the faces hewn out of Mt. Rushmore, which he resembles. For years he has presided over a Sunday night show of amazing durability, although his chief contribution to the proceedings has been mostly point-ing at acts and introducing bowling champions and channel swimmers in the audience.

Although he has spent years surrounded by acrobats, Ed's personality has remained unbending. Joe E. Lewis claims that

56

Sullivan was formerly a greeter at Forest Lawn Cemetery but had to give it up because they kept trying to bury him.

Despite his stiff personality, Ed has attracted big audiences year after year. He is never happier than when he is surrounded by a glee club of fifty voices, or sixty ballet dancers flinging themselves around the stage.

This makes it hard for him to top himself. Jack E. Leonard once said that Ed was going to bring back the Russian ballet and that for an encore they were going to bomb the theater.

I had always liked Ed and considered him a good friend. Therefore I was amazed to pick up my newspaper one day and read that he had "declared war on the Paar show."

He was tired of paying performers $5,000 or $7,500 on his show, Ed announced, only to have them turn around and appear on my program for $320, which is all we are able to pay anyone on our limited budget. Consequently, he had notified the big talent agencies that any top performer who went on our show for $320 would in the future get only $320 from him.

The ultimatum was issued after Sam Levenson, who gets $7,500 for his appearances on the Sullivan Show, appeared on our show for the customary $320. Myron Cohen, who was scheduled to appear on my show that night, suddenly cancelled and holed up incommunicado in his country home. Sam Levenson, who was also slated to appear again, likewise went AWOL.

I really couldn't blame Myron and Sam, as both were longtime regulars on the Sullivan Show, but their sudden cancellations underlined the performer's dilemma in the situation. Other performers, however, rallied round. Joey Bishop, Robert Merrill, Buddy Hackett and Joey Carter all rushed to our show the night of Sullivan's great ukase. Although their appearance endangered the chances of their going on with Ed in the future, they treated the matter lightheartedly.

"I've been on this show for two years and I have one gripe," Joey Bishop announced when he came on. "You told me

Sullivan only paid eighty dollars. I thought *this* was the big money."

Noting that New York was preparing to celebrate St. Patrick's Day, Joey added, "If you've got any guts, you'll yell, 'Down with Sullivan' when the St. Patrick's Day Parade goes by."

When I had to interrupt Joey to give the commercial for Bromo Seltzer, he eyed the headache remedy and cracked, "I wouldn't sell it. I'd take it."

Buddy Hackett told me he had never appeared on the Sullivan show and I asked why.

"I don't know," the rotund comic confessed. "Maybe Ed Sullivan just doesn't like round-faced men. He's never had Herbert Hoover on, either."

Although my guests treated Sullivan's threat with humor, actually a serious principle was involved. By threatening performers with economic reprisals for appearing on my program, Sullivan was, in effect, instituting a boycott. Also, he was dictating how another show should be run.

He didn't mind if big stars came on our show for $320, Ed grandly conceded, so long as they just chatted and didn't actually perform. It was all right by Ed if a famous singer like Robert Merrill came on for $320, as long as he didn't sing. But that still left some questions unanswered. Just where were we to draw the line? Was it all right if Robert Merrill hummed? If a fire-eater came on our show, would it be all right if he smoked?

Sullivan's position obviously seemed unfair. If Ed could dictate who could come on our show, then he could do the same to other shows. Besides, there was no reason why both programs should pay performers the same fee, because there is no comparison between the two programs.

Ed's show is one hour, once a week, in prime time, at eight o'clock Sunday nights. My effort is an hour and three-quarters each weekday night, with time out to remove the wounded.

Ed's show has an estimated audience of thirty-four million, mine an estimated eight million nightly. Ed has a budget of $110,000 for his one hour; our budget is $52,715 for nearly nine hours weekly, including the paper clips, which we re-use.

Ed himself modestly describes his program as a "rilly, rilly big shew." Ours has been rather aptly described as "an accident looking for someplace to happen."

Many big stars seemed more warm and appealing in the relaxed, informal atmosphere of our show than doing elaborately written and rehearsed routines on their own shows which, I feel, explained why we could get stars like Bob Hope, Red Skelton, Jack Benny, Jerry Lewis and many others. Even Ed Sullivan, it seemed to me, appeared more warm and human on our show, when he was a guest, than he did on his own.

What his boycott meant, I pointed out to Sullivan, was that performers had to choose between Ed's money and my friendship—and it wasn't fair to force such a decision on them. Many top performers, like Shelley Berman, Bob Newhart, and Elaine May and Mike Nichols had been discovered on our show and gone on to the big money on Ed's program. It didn't seem right to then tell them that they couldn't go back to the show that first brought them to his attention.

Performers were put in an agonizing position when newspaper reporters asked them point blank whom they were lining up with, although the question didn't bother Jack Douglas, the dead-panned wit who for years wrote for me and is now a highly successful nightclub comedian.

"I'd go on the Sullivan show any time for $320," he observed. "That's more than he's been willing to pay me up to now."

I then challenged Sullivan to let me go on opposite him on Sunday night and let the public decide, through the rating, whose stand they agreed with. I was heartened by the response to my proposal. Thousands of people wrote and wired their support.

A group in Erie, Pennsylvania, wired: "You are like a tea bag. You don't know your own strength until you get in hot water."

Keeping a stiff upper face, Sullivan declined my suggestion of a Sunday night rating battle but proposed, instead, that he come on my show and debate the issue. He asked that there be no audience, however, adding, in what some observers felt was an understatement, "I'm no performer."

Despite Ed's modesty about his abilities as an entertainer, he has a long record of public brawls and figured to be a formidable foe. He has clashed in the past with such opponents as Walter Winchell, Arthur Godfrey, Kate Smith and even Hedda Hopper, whom he said "serves no other function than playing housemother on Conrad Hilton junkets." At least two of these feuds, incidentally, were touched off by his forcing stars off other shows if they wanted to appear on his.

I welcomed the opportunity, however, and expressed the hope that his appearance on our show, for a meager $320, would not bar him from his own program. Our representatives got together to work out the ground rules and there were various suggestions for moderator, including Jackie Gleason, who would have undeniably lent weight to the proceedings.

Jackie demanded $7,820 to serve, and when asked how he arrived at that figure replied, "Seven thousand, five hundred from Sullivan. And three hundred and twenty from Paar."

I left the selection of moderator entirely up to Sullivan, who chose Bennett Cerf, the eminent publisher and punster. Ed's emissaries arrived at Cerf's office with a list of conditions longer than *Gone with the Wind*. Sullivan specified no commercials, no reaction shots, no applause, no talk about the debate before or after we came on. The tape was to be destroyed immediately after one airing. He also insisted on bringing his own makeup man, lighting director, prompting man and equipment, as well as his producer and his lawyer.

I agreed to all of this.

However, there was one point at which I drew the line. Under his proposal, Ed would make an opening statement. Then I would make a statement. Then he would make a brief rebuttal.

That wasn't my idea of a debate, which is defined by Webster as: "to discuss opposing reasons; argue. To dispute about, to argue formally. Discussion of opposing reasons; argument."

I didn't care if Ed read his statement off a prompting device so long as we had an opportunity to also argue the issue openly in free discussion.

At my insistence on this one point—after I had agreed to all of his many other demands—Ed retired in a pout, called off the debate and, in a masterpiece of garbled logic, announced that I was afraid to meet him.

"I have nothing to discuss with Paar," Ed declared loftily. "There is no subject here open to debate."

Since I was in the studio impatiently awaiting the fray, and Ed was sulking in his hotel suite, I had difficulty picturing myself as the one who was running away.

It seems to me that I won the argument by default. Perhaps my position was best defined by Morris Ernst, the noted lawyer, who said, "It's as if Macy's told Bennett Cerf that if he sold books to Gimbels they wouldn't handle them. If Sullivan succeeds in his announced course, the public will lose its rights under the First Amendment. Such tactics can only muddy the free marketplace of ideas, entertainment and education which television is licensed to provide."

I lost the battle in the newspapers as usual. Columnists have a highly developed herd instinct and tangling with one is like shooting a cop—you bring the whole lot of them down on your head.

Although Ed started the whole rhubarb by hurling his ultimatum at the talent agencies and I merely spoke up for the performers who were caught in the middle, I came off sounding like Jack the Ripper. The pictures which the papers ran of me looked like passport photos, while in almost every picture Ed, who smiles so seldom he looks like a disbarred Good Humor Man, was always beaming a benign smile.

Many papers suggested that the whole thing was a publicity stunt. If it was—which it most certainly wasn't—the papers were idiotic to be taken in so completely. And if it was on the up and up, a serious dispute over a principle, they were still wrong to give it the exaggerated attention they did.

When the smoke had cleared, most papers said that the attention given the whole incident was ridiculous. I agree. I think it was absurd to devote headlines and front pages to a dispute between two entertainers, if I may use the word loosely, at a time when there was a crisis in Laos, fighting in the Congo, a recession in this country and various other serious problems.

Yet who gave our little intramural scuffle all the notoriety? The newspapers! Who ran the stories on front pages and plastered headlines on them? The newspapers! TV itself paid scant attention to the rumpus. My own network made only a wry passing mention of our squabble on the Huntley-Brinkley news. The papers played it to the hilt.

There's an old saying that it doesn't matter what the papers print about you—so long as they spell your name right. In this instance what the papers printed was almost entirely derogatory, but most of them did manage to spell Paar with two *a*'s. When they were all through, our show had its highest rating in history.

Ed and I finally agreed on a cease-fire, and all is now calm between us. The cessation of hostilities was arranged by Jack Benny, who sprang his truce proposal out of the blue one night on the show.

"Sometimes I think you're absolutely nuts," Jack declared, and began lecturing me like a Dutch uncle on the folly of getting involved in public brawls. "If you're going to be mad at someone, be mad at Eichmann," Jack suggested.

As I listened to the stern lecture from Benny, who launched me in network radio and to whom I am devoted, I began to feel like Mickey Rooney being rebuked by Judge Hardy in the old *Andy Hardy* series.

Jack wound up by demanding that I tell the audience I was sorry. I hesitated, but Jack was brandishing his violin over my head so I thought I'd better. It wasn't that I was afraid he'd hit me with the violin. I was afraid he'd play it.

9

The Press Mess

I HAPPENED TO GLANCE at a newspaper not long ago, while lining the bottom of our birdcage with it, and I was struck by its crusading tone. This set me to thinking. Aroused by this editorial fervor, I retrieved other papers, one in which I had wrapped the garbage, and another I had put in the garage for our dachshund to sleep on.

The causes were a little hard to determine sometimes, and I had to wade through pages of hatchet slayings, colorful divorces and breathless accounts of Tuesday Weld's latest romantic flurries, but the editorials were all angry about something.

One was denouncing inefficiency in the New York school system. Another was pointing with alarm at excessive violence on television. Still another was inveighing against our foreign policy. Not only were the editorial pages all up in arms, but almost every page bristled with critics all explaining what was wrong with practically everything.

Washington columnists told what we were doing wrong in Laos and Berlin. Dorothy Kilgallen was telling the State Department what we did wrong in Cuba with the same intensity that she reported that Bobby Darrin and Sandra Dee were acting silly again. Drama critics explained what was wrong with Tennessee Williams. Sports columnists analyzed what was wrong with Mickey Mantle's swing. In just one day's papers, I discovered, I could find out what was wrong about almost anything under the sun.

Except newspapers.

For some reason it's hard to find anything adverse about newspapers in the press . . . even if someone gets up in public and says it. Not long ago Cecil Harmsworth King, the biggest publisher in the world, held a press conference in New York during which he criticized American newspapers. Mr. King's credentials as a critic of the press are considerable. He owns several British newspapers including the *London Daily Mirror,* the largest paper in the world. In addition, he publishes at least two-thirds of all the magazines published in England, along with numerous books. So his views on journalism are worth listening to.

This, in part, is what Mr. King had to say about American newspapers: "They consist of acres of soggy verbiage, cubic miles of repetition, headlines incredibly amateurish, layout non-existent, handling of pictures ludicrous." The main fault of our papers, he went on, is "brevity—lack of."

Avidly I thumbed through our papers the next day to see how they handled this critique by a noted publisher, but all in vain. There was space for almost everything else. The Supreme Court had overruled the conviction of the Apalachin mobsters, but the police had routed the folk singers in Greenwich Village. Walter Winchell was warning not to invite Bernard Baruch and Evelyn Rudie to the same party. And in Nick Kenny's column I read a cheerful little poem that left me depressed all day.

All the other big news was in the papers, but nothing on Mr. King and his low opinion of our press. For all the attention his opinions got, the British publisher might just as well have yelled them down a rain barrel.

Although there were reporters galore at his press conference, not a line about it appeared in New York newspapers the next day. Eventually a few brief stories did turn up—mostly in the publishing trade press. That was all. The American press as a whole was so quiet you could have heard a cliché drop.

I don't have Mr. King's formidable qualifications for criticizing the American press, but it's nice to have him join me in my little war with the newspapers. In fact, I really haven't any special qualifications for acting as a critic of the press except one: I'm willing to do it and practically no one else seems to want the job, for which I can't say I blame them. Let anyone criticize some aspect of the press, or some of its practitioners, and some newspapers will retaliate with slanted stories, bad angled photos or other snide tactics.

This is not true of all newspapers, of course, nor most newspaper people, but there are a few papers, and a few columnists, who indulge in slander by innuendo and other hatchet methods. Columnists like Walter Winchell, the pioneer of the three-dot or fly-speck school of journalism, and Dorothy Kilgallen, the masked marvel of TV, have weapons in their columns, and actors have always shrunk from incurring their wrath. True, columnists have had their intramural feuds— Sidney Skolsky once bit Louella Parsons in the arm—but not since Rudolph Valentino challenged a movie critic to a duel have actors struck back at their tormentors until I took up the cudgels.

I first encountered this small reign of terror in Hollywood, after World War II, where I found most of the film colony cowering before the massed might of two little trade papers and a brace of lady movie columnists, once identified by Marlon Brando as "the fat one and the one with the hats."

Having survived such wartime terrors as athlete's foot, Spam and typhoid shots, I did not feel intimidated by either Louella Parsons, a veteran foe of the English language, or Hedda Hopper, whose trademark is a giddy profusion of millinery which prompted a friend of mine to sigh, "All those hats and only two heads!"

My first actual skirmish with a newspaper came when I wrote a protesting letter to a trade paper which had run an item that H. B. Warner, the star of *King of Kings,* was "now starring in the unemployment line." I had never met Mr.

Warner but I wrote the paper that it hardly became a publication which existed on the advertising of show people to humiliate a fine actor who had encountered financial adversity.

The paper didn't take kindly to my critique and began panning the radio show I was doing and making slighting personal references about me. I fired back with heated letters to the editor. When he wouldn't print my letters, while continuing to needle me in his columns, I began buying full-page ads in a rival trade paper to have my say about his publication. This expensive brand of self-expression, which had begun over an item about an actor in the unemployment line, ended when my show was cancelled and I found *myself* in the unemployment line.

Broke and discouraged, I fled Hollywood in a departure reminiscent of Napoleon's retreat from Moscow. The state of employment in New York was better, and I landed a TV show on C.B.S., but the state of journalism was just as bad.

Performers in New York lived in the same dread of certain columnists, I found, and the East Coast franchise for character assassination was held by Walter Winchell, a yipping, pistol-packing, fire-chasing, posturing, pontificating, frenzied ex-hoofer.

Winchell, who broadcast with his hat on, apparently under the assumption he was appearing on color radio, has a penchant for mangling words and reputations which enables him to bully actors and others in the public eye. His column is made up largely of trivia contributed by press agents who will go to any length, including fiction, to get their clients mentioned.

According to Broadway legend, one press agent once got the lead in Winchell's column by hinting that a well-known actress had cancer. The actress, who never felt better, was naturally indignant. She submitted X rays, doctors' reports and other evidence of her good health, together with a demand from her lawyer that Winchell retract the story.

Winchell immediately began his own research to find out if the actress was really ill, and whether to wreak vengeance on her or the press agent who had given him the item. This struck terror in the hearts of Broadway press agents. For days they waited in trepidation to see on whose head Winchell's wrath would fall.

One night a group of the nervous press agents were speculating over the ominous situation.

"All I can say," one of them muttered gloomily, "is that if that girl hasn't really got cancer, she sure is in a lot of trouble with Winchell."

The days when cancer was considered less dangerous than Winchell's wrath are happily ended, and of late years he seems even less particular about where he gets items. This interesting fact was disclosed during the government action against Alexander Guterma, a former president of the Mutual Broadcasting System, for failure to register as a foreign agent.

According to testimony at the Justice Department action, Guterma entered into an unusual agreement with representatives of dictator Rafael Trujillo. For $750,000, to be paid in advance, Guterma agreed that over an eighteen-month period the Mutual network would broadcast a "monthly minimum of 425 minutes of news and commentary regarding the Dominican Republic."

Otto Vega, special assistant to Trujillo, testified that at a meeting attended by Hal Roach, Jr., and Porfirio Rubirosa, the international lover boy, Guterma offered a demonstration of how the secret propaganda scheme would work. According to Vega's testimony, Guterma asked him for a sample of some news he would like broadcast.

When Vega said he didn't have anything, Guterma said, according to Vega, "Well, since we have Mr. Rubirosa here and Mr. Roach here, why not say Mr. Rubirosa is going to make a picture for Hal Roach in the Dominican Republic and they are busy negotiating that?"

The very next day, Vega said, returning to New York in Guterma's private plane, the group heard Walter Winchell recite their make-believe news item over the Mutual network.

Lately Winchell has confessed that even he is getting tired of his column. "I doubt if I will ever get the kick again," he wrote in a rare moment of candor, "reporting three-dot trivia about Lizzie Tish being that way about Joe Phluggy. It now seems all 'so-whattish.' "

The days when Winchell's column could frighten performers are now long gone and, looking back, I'm sorry I ever got into a ruckus with him. I did it because I thought his influence was a threat to actors, when actually it was dying a natural death. When I began rapping him on our show it focused attention on him all over again.

A friend called me one day and pointed this out. "His career was dying and you gave it artificial respiration," my friend said. "Your reviving Winchell was the biggest feat of resurrection since Lazarus was raised from the dead."

Although Winchell no longer seems to exert any influence over performers, unfortunately he has left his mark, or perhaps scar is a better word, on the profession.

The New Yorker magazine, in a profile on Winchell, said that his prying brand of privacy-invading journalism has infected all other journalists in some way. Winchell, the magazine said, has been responsible for lowering individual privacy throughout the whole field of journalism.

Ironically, although his radio and TV shows sank in a sea of public apathy, the type of peeping-Tom journalism he spawned in his column has spread.

The most virulent form of this kind of misrepresentation appears in fan magazines. These periodicals, which used to be so saccharine as to invite diabetes, have suddenly become as racy as the Kinsey Report.

Most actors used to grudgingly put up with the magazines' tireless invasion of their privacy, as long as they printed nothing worse than stories as gooey as melted marshmallows, but of late they have been rebelling against the outrageous misrepresentation, and high time. Elizabeth Taylor and Eddie Fisher have slapped a group of fan magazines with a suit for $17,250,000, which I hope will serve as a deterrent in the fan magazines' wholesale campaign of slander by suggestion.

Here are samples of some magazines' headlines, with an explanation of what the stories were *really* about:

LIZ-EDDIE-DEBBIE—
ARE THEY PLANNING TO LIVE TOGETHER?

(This one said that Debbie Reynolds *might* buy a home in Jamaica, and that the Fishers also *might*.)

EDDIE NAMED FATHER OF LIZ'S CHILD!

(The story reported that Eddie Fisher had legally adopted Liza Todd, Liz Taylor's daughter by the late Mike Todd.)

STEVE BOYD HAS BROKEN UP
LIZ'S AND EDDIE'S MARRIAGE

(The article pointed out that Stephen Boyd, who was to appear with Miss Taylor in *Cleopatra,* often has romanced with his leading ladies, and that it *could* happen again. The picture hadn't even gone into production when the story appeared.)

"We appealed to several magazines to put an end to such false stories when they began affecting our children's lives as well as our own," the Fishers said in their suit. "These appeals had no effect. We respect the press's right to cover our activities, but some magazines are not interested in reporting as much as distorting."

I was delighted to see the Fishers taking legal action to stop this kind of distortion. I was also pleased when Liberace won a libel suit against a London paper whose columnist had written a vicious attack on him. It is good to see performers striking back.

It's encouraging, too, to note that a few other hardy souls have joined in what seemed for a long time to be my own private war. Several prominent Americans have lately taken pot shots at the press, including some from within the ranks of journalism.

Charles Collingwood, an old companion from the C.B.S. *Morning Show,* has a local program reviewing the press. A. J. Liebling, one of the country's finest reporters, occasionally grumbles in *The New Yorker* about the state of the wayward press. William E. Evjue, a crusading Wisconsin editor, recently resigned from the American Society of Newspaper Editors charging that the American press had failed to meet its responsibilities.

Robert Moses, New York's blunt Parks Commissioner, charges that the "yellow press" is worse than ever before in history, and that it is driving dedicated people out of public service by "baseless mud-throwing." And one of the strongest blasts came from Robert Estabrook, of the *Washington Post and Times Herald,* who suggested that newspapers that smoulder indignantly over the transgressions of others might well take a good look at their own.

"Our indignation would be better founded," he wrote, "if we also managed to muster a few olfactory shudders about the garbage in our own backyard."

It's nice suddenly to have such strong support in my long contention that our newspapers are not above reproach. Lately even John Crosby, the nationally syndicated columnist, has taken to expressing his disillusion with the press, and I want to welcome him to the club. John is a belated convert, who achieved cynicism about the Fourth Estate rather late in life, but we trust he will be a faithful recruit.

A couple of years ago John wrote a column charging that broadcasting lacked the freedom of journalism. "In radio and television," he declared, "stars like Jack Paar live under the immediate and intimate control of their advertisers. The newspaper tradition is freedom to observe and report the facts as they are. It's the tradition of freedom that people like Paar can't understand because they've never had any."

At the time I replied that Crosby's charge that I was controlled by sponsors was ridiculous, and cited chapter and verse on my relations with sponsors which embraced more dissenting opinions by me than were ever handed down by even Chief Justice Oliver Wendell Holmes, the "great dissenter." However, if John Crosby was not convinced by my arguments about who has more freedom, he seems to have been by subsequent events.

When Newton Minow, the newly appointed chairman of the Federal Communications Commission, made a speech to the National Association of Broadcasters criticizing TV programming as a "vast wasteland," Crosby wrote two columns praising Minow for his stand and criticizing TV and broadcaster pressure groups. The *New York Herald Tribune* syndicate, which distributes Crosby's column, promptly ordered the two columns killed.

Ironically, the order went out at almost the exact time that John Hay Whitney, publisher of the *Herald Tribune,* was addressing the country's promotion executives and expressing fears over the possible New Frontier threats to the freedom of the press!

The publishing industry in the United States turns out approximately twenty trillion words a day, and I shudder to think how many of them are wrong. I like to collect the more spectacular boners I run across, and always have quite an impressive collection, although they pile up so fast that Miriam keeps throwing them out lest I get trapped in a maze of old newspapers like the Collier brothers.

One of my faithful contributors is Louella Parsons. Not long ago Louella gave me quite a start when she reported that my old friend, Dudley Field Malone, the famous lawyer who played Winston Churchill in a movie, was "holding court in the Hollywood Brown Derby." The reason I was startled at this announcement was that Malone had died more than ten years before.

However, Louella evened the score a few days later when she referred to Joseph Breen, the former head of the Hollywood Production Code Authority, as "the late Joseph Breen," although Mr. Breen was very much alive.

Miss Parsons writes her syndicated column for the Hearst papers and for some reason they turn up with some of the funniest boners. Charles Collingwood called my attention to one fine array, the occasion a birthday party for Anna Maria Alberghetti, the star of the Broadway musical, *Carnival*.

Hearst's New York *Journal American* took particular note of the occasion. On page fourteen, Cholly Knickerbocker wrote: "Quite a number of top names cut out early to attend the *twenty-fourth* birthday party for Anna Maria Alberghetti."

Further on, there was a pretty picture of the young star with the caption—"Actress-singer Anna Maria Alberghetti, star of the Broadway musical *Carnival,* about to blow out the candles on her *twenty-fifth* birthday cake."

And on page seventeen, the ever-reliable Louella Parsons observed, "Anna, who was celebrating her *twenty-sixth* birthday, has matured greatly since her big success on Broadway."

She's matured greatly, all right. She aged two years between pages fourteen and seventeen of the *Journal American!*

These errors aren't very earth-shaking, I admit, but it makes you wonder: if papers can be so wrong about little things, how accurate can they be in reporting really important events? Someone once said that when you hear two different accounts of an auto accident it makes you wonder about history, and when I read two different newspapers it makes me wonder about the present.

Sometimes the errors of the press are simple human mistakes, like the fumbling of Miss Alberghetti's age, but at other times papers seem to go out of their way to concoct some boner. On April 13, 1961, I read in the afternoon *Journal American* that Sir Winston Churchill had departed from New York by plane for London.

"As his plane roared off the runway," the paper wrote, "it climaxed a sentimental journey which the old warrior surely must have deemed a great personal triumph." The account went into some detail about Sir Winston's departure, ending with—"Mr. Churchill and his party motored to the airport from Aristotle Onassis' yacht, anchored in the Hudson River off Seventy-ninth Street."

It was a sentimental story, and it almost brought tears to my eyes, but there was one flaw in it. Mr. Churchill was still aboard the yacht in the middle of the Hudson River!

I had driven by a few hours earlier, in a heavy storm, and learned that Mr. Churchill and his party were marooned aboard by fierce winds and choppy water. It wasn't until the following day that he actually left.

However, perhaps all this serves one useful purpose, as Samuel Butler pointed out. "The greatest service that newspapers perform," he wrote, "is to teach us to view the printed word with suspicion."

My differences with the press have rarely involved critics, whose right to pass judgment on me or any other performer I have never questioned. Time was when I agreed with Brendan Behan, who told me a critic is like a eunuch in a harem—he's in the midst of something exciting but he can take no part in it.

All this is changing of late, though, and critics are rushing before cameras in such abundance that you can scarcely manage to miss one if you turn on your set, although I always try.

John Crosby has had a couple of TV shows sunk under him. Harriet Van Horn bobs up occasionally on a panel show. Marie Torre does a local TV show in New York. Now Terrance O'Flaherty of the *San Francisco Chronicle* has turned up opposite our bedtime follies on the program called *P.M. East/P.M. West*.

When John Crosby took to TV, critic O'Flaherty said he thought it was a mistake. I agree. I think it was also a mistake when O'Flaherty took to television. It seemed like a much better arrangement when TV critics just wrote columns analyzing all that was wrong with us performers, instead of going on television themselves. It makes us all look good by comparison.

In the sporadic warfare between columnists and performers, I feel that the last word was said by Tallulah Bankhead. Tallulah once complained to me that Earl Wilson had written in his column that when she wanted her guests to leave she simply started taking off her clothes.

Tallulah phoned Wilson and indignantly denied the item. "In the first place, dahling, I haven't got the figure for it," she trumpeted. "In the second place, if I want to get rid of my guests I just read them your column."

10

Lost in a Vast Wasteland

TELEVISION is getting its lumps these days.

As this is written, the industry has recently been investigated by Congress and the Federal Communications Commission. Chairman Newton Minow of the F.C.C. has described television as a "vast wasteland," prompting one viewer to write in complaining that he couldn't find that new western, *Vast Wasteland,* on any channel.

Practically everyone seems to be complaining about TV except the people—who go right on staring at it as if hypnotized.

Fred Allen always complained that TV was called a medium because nothing on it was ever well done. British playwright Shelagh Delaney claims that there are only two kinds of TV in America—"awful bloody and bloody awful." And David Susskind, whom Oscar Levant once described as sounding like "salami dipped in chicken fat," charged in a typical, jaw-breaking triple-metaphor that today's TV fare was "celluloid sausage coming down the pike by the ream."

Well, I'd like to rise to say a few kind words on behalf of my beleaguered medium. Television has its shortcomings, to be sure, and I've done some complaining about them myself from time to time, but I don't think the critics I've listened to have the cure.

Judging from the *Ev and Charley Show,* starring those two grand old troupers, Senator Everett Dirksen and Congressman Charles Halleck, the Gallagher and Shean of Capitol Hill, I don't think that Congress can improve television. Nor do I think Newton Minow can make his "vast wasteland" bloom, no matter how well watered it is with the tears of critics.

The cure, dear reader, as they used to say in Victorian novels, lies with you.

Even before television, H. L. Mencken observed that no one ever went broke underestimating the taste of the American public, and TV has confirmed the soundness of his judgment. Television has frequently put on fine programs, only to have the viewing public ignore them. When the American Broadcasting Company, which had been criticized for putting on mostly westerns and private-eye shows, finally ran the costly and distinguished series based on the life of Sir Winston Churchill, it was clobbered in the ratings by *What's My Line?* and Ralph Edwards' *This Is Your Life*.

The talents of Sid Caesar and Paddy Chayefsky and Jackie Gleason have departed the home screens because the public didn't care. Apparently people would just as soon watch *Hawaiian Eye* and Lawrence Welk. The "Golden Age of Television" turned to dross when the fine original dramas of the mid 1950's gave way to the assembly-line, machine-tooled series ground out by the Hollywood film factories. Why should television lavish a vast amount of money on bringing *Oedipus Rex* or the Moiseyev Dancers to the public when it is just as happy watching something like *The Price Is Right* or *Candid Camera?* The majority of viewers seem happy with TV as it is—and that's what keeps it the way it is.

Surveys show that there are more TV sets than bathtubs in U.S. homes, and that the average American spends one hundred and thirty-one minutes daily in front of them. The A.C. Nielsen Company says that Americans spend more time watching TV than doing anything but sleeping. Children spend so much time watching TV that they are changing from irresistible forces into immovable objects.

A Brooklyn sociologist, Dr. Clara Appell, made a survey of TV's effect on the home and discovered that it drastically affects not only the eating and sleeping schedules of families, but even the sex life of married couples. Dr. Appell says that she found an increase in sexual activity due to married couples being carried away by romantic scenes on the old movies late at night.

However, my own Paar poll, taken among people who insist on accosting me on the street, shows there is a lessening in marital relations among couples who watch my show since often one partner insists on sitting glued to the set while the other wends his or her way to bed alone.

Compulsive TV watching is not confined to this country. The fact that even in England people will watch anything on television is illustrated by a story told me by Michael Flanders, the British actor. Flanders says that he once went to the beach at Brighton and found it almost deserted. Investigating, he found the crowd that usually sunned and swam at the beach were all inside a big tent watching television.

Being shown were scenes shot at the beach at Brighton.

Perhaps the biggest accusation levelled against television is excessive violence. However, I can't get as exercised as Congress over violence on TV because it seems to me there's more of it in the newspapers or on the television news shows than on *Gunsmoke* or *The Untouchables*. The good guys usually win, in the end, on those shows, but not on the Huntley-Brinkley News. Life, alas, seems to be violent.

The worst thing about television, in my opinion, is not excessive sex and violence or even its overabundance of commercials, but its strange taboos. One series once banned a drama on Lincoln, because it was sponsored by an automotive company of a different name, and the General Electric dramatic hour is reported to have wanted to change the title of Kipling's *The Light That Failed*. Everyone seems to want to steer clear of controversy and David Susskind complains that the medium may be reduced to producing only "happy plays for happy people with happy problems."

I once got mixed up in this kind of foolishness when I was doing the *Camel Caravan* show on radio. I did a monologue saying that our scientific achievements had not made us happier or more secure. "Now that man can fly through the air like a bird," I said, "and swim in the sea like a fish, wouldn't it be wonderful if he could just walk the earth like a man?"

An advertising man rushed up to me in rehearsal and said I couldn't use the line. "Why not?" I demanded.

"It's anti-Russian," he said. "They call Russia the 'bear that walks like a man.'"

Sponsors still tip-toe around in fear of inadvertently offending some racial group and it's become a problem to know who to make the bad guys on TV shows. It used to be easy during World War II, when all you had to do was make the villains Germans or Japanese. Now, however, the Germans and Japanese are our buddies, while our wartime allies—the Russians and Chinese—are the bad guys.

All of this makes things pretty confusing in some of the old movies on *The Late Late Show*.

Local pride is always a touchy subject, and I have managed to offend various cities and states, but racial groups are the most easily offended of all. "It's getting to a point," writer Gore Vidal has complained, "where the only murderer to be depicted on television will be a white Protestant fiend, preferably named Adams."

The Italians seem particularly sensitive and have raised a loud outcry about the many gangsters with Italian names on *The Untouchables* and other TV shows based on the Capone gang era of the 1920's. Italian groups protested so vigorously, in fact, that *The Untouchables* has agreed in the future not to portray gangsters with Italian names.

"A better solution," my friend Jack Douglas claims, "might be to have the real gangsters change *their* names."

TV is so bad, Alex King grumbled recently, that people are reduced to talking to each other again. But nobody seems to listen anymore. Everyone seems to be writing books, but nobody is reading them. Everyone is talking and no one is listening. Listening is becoming a lost art, like the manufacture of buggy whips.

I've noticed this trend especially in radio and television interviews. A lot of the interviewers get so interested in their own questions that they answer them themselves, while the hapless interviewee sits by hoping to get a word in eventually. It's a form of enchantment with the sound of one's own voice that affects almost everyone, but is especially virulent among broadcasting interviewers.

I have been observing the foibles of my broadcasting brethren since my days as a young radio announcer, and I have an interesting casebook. Those were the days of the big dance bands on radio, and an announcer's greatest moment of glory, in cities like Cleveland and Buffalo, where I worked, came when he got to introduce the band members on remote broadcasts from a local hotel or ballroom.

We used to cup our hands to our ears, the better to hear the dulcet tones of our own voices, and announce, "Now our vocalist steps up to the microphone to ask the musical question—'How Deep Is the Ocean?' " Or "Now we hear the musical lament—'Why Do I Love You?' "

That fancy-Dan language looks a little silly now, but at least it made sense. Disc jockeys, I notice, are still using such introductions, but half the time they don't make any sense at all. Not long ago I heard a disc jockey say, "Now, here is Pat Boone to ask the musical question—'Cecelia?' "

I don't know where the question enters here, unless there's something we don't know about Cecelia.

Recently I heard the introduction to end all musical introductions. "Now, here is Julius LaRosa to ask the musical question—'Funiculi, Funicula?' "

While disc jockeys don't seem to listen to themselves, TV interviewers often don't listen to the guests they are interviewing. They ask a question and then sit with an absent-minded expression trying desperately to think up their next witticism, regardless of its bearing on the answer their inter-viewee is giving.

They are never at a loss for words, however, since they use the expression "That's wunnerful" to cover almost any con-tingency. Once I saw a program which had as its guest a pa-tient in an iron lung. The announcer asked how the iron lung worked and the attending nurse explained its operation, say-ing that if the electric power should go off the patient would die.

"Oh, that's wunnerful," beamed the announcer.

Another time I watched a famous singing comedienne on a charity telethon. "I've been up all night," she croaked, "and my voice is nearly gone. But I want to sing 'My Funny Valen-tine' and dedicate it to all these fabulous paraplegic kids."

But perhaps the best example of the nonlistening inter-viewer is Les Paul's story of an interview on a Hollywood TV station with Cornelius Vanderbilt, Jr., the globe-trotting journalist. The interview got off well enough and was pro-gressing nicely, when the announcer asked Vanderbilt about his most exciting experience.

"It was during World War II," the journalist said, "and I was covering the fighting on the Russian front. One day I was captured by Russian troops. I was thrown into an armored car and driven wildly through the night to an unknown destination.

"When I was dragged out of the car I was stunned to see we were at the Kremlin. My captors hauled me into that for-bidding bastion, down a long, gloomy corridor, and finally hurled me to the floor. Looking up I saw Stalin glowering down at me!"

At this point Vanderbilt paused for breath in his harrow-ing story.

"I see," said the nervous announcer. "Do you have any hobbies?"

11

Discoveries in the Dark

WHEN I STARTED on the *Tonight* show the critics looked on the relationship as a Hollywood marriage. They said it would never last. I didn't feel too confident myself and for the first several months I used to leave my car at the stage door with the motor running. Now, nearly five years and several lawsuits later, the show is still going strong although I'm beginning to feel a little winded.

In those nearly five years, comedy has undergone some exciting and significant changes. A whole new crop of talented newcomers has risen to stardom and the thing that I'm proudest of about our show is that it introduced many of these fresh new talents to the national television audience for the first time.

Shelley Berman, Mike Nichols and Elaine May, Bob Newhart, Phil Ford and Mimi Hines, Pat Harrington, Jr. and Jack Douglas all made their TV debuts on our conversation klatsch.

So did such lively ladies as Geneviève, Dody Goodman, Carol Burnett, Peggy Cass, Phyllis Diller and Selma Diamond.

Joey Bishop, Buddy Hackett, Jonathan Winters and Charley Weaver were seasoned performers but had not achieved the national recognition they deserved until our program exposed their talents to a mass audience.

We also feel fortunate to have been able to provide a long overdue introduction for the young Negro comedians, including Dick Gregory and Nipsey Russell, who introduced adult Negro humor to the American scene.

We brought literate and stimulating conversation into American homes, with great conversationalists like Alexander King, Peter Ustinov and Robert Morley.

In our quest for new faces we found talent in the strangest places. Many of those who have become nationally popular weren't even entertainers. Alex King was an artist and writer. Pat Harrington, Jr., was a time salesman at N.B.C. Phyllis Diller was a housewife with five kids before she decided she liked to be funny.

The amazing thing is the manner in which the new medium of television made unknown youngsters into stars overnight. Bob Hope and Danny Thomas and Red Skelton worked years in vaudeville and clubs before achieving stardom, while Shelley Berman and Bob Newhart did it overnight.

When Shelley Berman, an ex-cab driver and dance instructor from Chicago, who had been playing small clubs, was booked for our show the first time he had to get his money in advance as he was flat broke. A few months later he was making $500,000 a year and had three managers, a lawyer, an advance man, two secretaries, two press agents and a valet.

The greatest conversationalist I have ever met is Alexander King, a frail but fierce little man with the air of a delinquent leprechaun.

I first encountered Alex in January of 1959 and I'm sure that a more unlikely guest never presented himself to our program. He had written a book called *Mine Enemy Grows Older* and friends had told me he was an engaging if unpredictable conversationalist.

I was a bit startled when I met him backstage. He was a fragile man, about sixty, with a wispy mustache, a jaunty bow tie, a gentle smile and a satanic gleam in his eye. Then he sat down with me in front of the camera and began to talk. Like March, he came in like a lamb but went out like a lion. Rambling along in a stream-of-consciousness style, he was by turns witty, irreverent, poetic, outrageous and vitriolic.

He had absolutely no inhibitions about himself. He talked

freely and colorfully about his four wives, his drug addiction and his varied careers as artist, playwright and editor, peppering his conversation with invective and tipping over idols with obvious delight in his careening conversation.

Overnight he talked himself into a national institution. His book, which had sold 6,394 copies when he came on the show, sold 26,000 copies in the next week and shot to the top of the non-fiction best seller list. That was only the start. So strong was the impact of Alex's hobgoblin personality on the public that he quickly got his own TV show and promptly wrote another top best seller. He also was almost swallowed up in a tidal wave of mail including two letters offering him an extra kidney. (He presently gets along on one-eighth of one kidney.)

Now Hollywood is planning a movie on his life.

"I used to throw all this stuff away for nothing," he muses. "Now I get paid for it."

Noel Coward once remarked on how well he used the language. "I have to," said Alex. "I'm an immigrant."

Immigration, I reminded him, is the sincerest form of flattery.

Alex can talk entertainingly about almost anything because practically everything seems to have happened to him. Born in Vienna, he speaks five languages, has traveled extensively, and has had an astounding number of adventures and misadventures. On the show he has regaled the audience with accounts of serving as a midwife in North Africa, being jailed for stealing art from the Metropolitan Museum, serving as an editor of *Life* magazine, wearing nothing but pink ties for thirty years and nearly dying a half-dozen times from a formidable array of diseases.

His books, like his conversation, are grab bags of reminiscences, opinions, invective and bizarre and improbable tales that sometimes strain credulity but are never dull. "I notice," a friend told him recently, "that you didn't ruin your autobiography by putting your life into it."

To Alex, nothing is sacred. He has lit into Elsa Maxwell, the editors of *Life* magazine, the advertising business, art critics, and marriage.

His vituperative outbreaks have shocked many people including, on occasion, his pretty wife Margie who once suggested he needed a "little common censoring."

Yet although he is quick to tilt a lance, Alex's memories are frequently tender and poetic. "I am just a great big dragging anchor of nostalgia," he says, "hopelessly enmired in the pleasant, squidgy muck of my memories."

Many of his most colorful remembrances are of his days in New York's Greenwich Village. One night he was coming home to his apartment there when he saw a newspaperman he knew slightly get out of a cab with a big, homely dog. The man went into his apartment, leaving the dog to wander off down the street alone.

Indignant, Alex knocked on the man's door and asked, "How come you just walked off and left your dog?"

"He's not my dog," the man protested. "I never saw him before."

"He must be your dog," Alex insisted. "I saw him get out of the cab with you."

"I know," the man admitted. "I was coming home and I saw the dog and thought to myself: 'What chance has a big ugly dog like that of getting a ride in a cab?' So I hailed a cab and gave him a ride around the block."

As might be expected from someone married four times, Alex has some definite ideas on matrimony. "I was never married less than five years to anyone," he told me. "All of my ex-wives made enormously successful marriages. One of them told me I was just like a good finishing school."

After one marriage, he honeymooned at the Garden of Allah in Hollywood. One night he heard pounding on the wall coming from an adjoining room. Rushing next door he discovered the occupant, an actress named Peaches Del Monte, was trapped inside her glass shower. Gallantly Alex opened the jammed shower door and freed the dripping actress.

"I'm terribly sorry," he said, as she stepped out of the shower.

"What are you sorry for?" Peaches asked, reaching for a towel.

"I'm sorry," Alex smiled, "because I'm on my honeymoon."

Alex became so popular on our show that he got his own syndicated hour-long TV program with his young wife Margie. I asked him if he planned to interview guests to help fill the hour program. "I *loathe* guests," he said. "When other people talk it makes me nervous."

Because of this, Alex shuns cocktail parties which he thinks reduce conversation to babble. "There is no repartee—only 'departee,' " he says. "We think of what we should have said after we depart."

I once told Alex that I was going to give him a silver tongue on the anniversary of his first appearance. "Good," he said. "I can use it for a shoe horn."

Alex started life as an artist and one of his first jobs was painting Chinese murals in a kosher restaurant. He hates abstract painting. He once went to an exhibition where there were two canvases, both completely blank. "One of them won first prize," he said. "I don't know what the other guy did wrong."

Once I spoke to him of my youth. "When I was young," I recalled, "I wanted to be like Errol Flynn."

"So did Errol Flynn," observed Alex.

With his newly won affluence, Alex has now moved from his little walkup apartment in Greenwich Village to a Park Avenue apartment. There he spends his days, draped in a bathrobe, writing his endless reminiscences and his irascible opinions leaning on a breadboard which he holds in his lap. With three books all best sellers, he plans six more.

Ironically, at last when he can afford anything he wants,

his health is so delicate he can eat only rice. Yet he is happy. "I love to get up in the morning," he says. "I'm so delighted I'm still alive."

Once when he came to the show his face had a particularly ruddy glow and I remarked how healthy he looked. "I stooped over to tie my shoe lace," he said, "and all the blood rushed to my head."

Alex is extremely fastidious and has a fetish about washing his hands frequently. One night before the show he washed his hands and then went down to a drug store to get a cup of coffee. A grimy-looking workman, covered with grease, spotted Alex and said, "Mr. King, I'm a great fan of yours. May I just shake your hand?"

Alex, recoiling from the grimy outthrust hand, said, "Just hug me."

Despite his toy-terrier ferocity, there are moments when Alex shows alarming tendencies toward mellowness. Once I referred to him as an "angry man."

"I'm not," he said wistfully. "I love people and want to go out of this world loving them. I only get irritated with those who get in the way of that love."

His love is quite all-embracing and he admits to having four thousand intimate friends. "Wherever I go, people on the street recognize me," he told me. "I'm looked upon as everybody's unfettered libido rampant. If I were a young man I might be tempted to set up as an oracle, but anyone over sixty knows there are no safe charts in the world. The only advice I can give is, live each day as if it were your last day on this earth. It very well may be."

Buddy Hackett, the dumpling-shaped comedian, is a good example of the vicissitudes of show business. For years fellow comedians have known him as one of the most droll ad-libbers around. Yet in his own TV series, a couple of Broadway shows and several movies his reception was something less than overwhelming. The trouble with all those ventures was that people kept writing for Buddy and the material was never as funny as he is.

One night he came on our show and we just let him talk. He was so funny that everyone is once more trying to put him into movies, scripted TV series and Broadway shows so they can make him unfunny all over again.

Me, I like him the way he is—untamed and uninhibited. He needs plenty of elbow room in telling a story, and we try to give it to him. "This show is great," he told me. "It's the only place a Jew can go to Confession."

Buddy's humor, which is part sadness, derives mainly from his background as a poor Jewish boy. He learned his comedy in the "borscht belt" where so many comedians have gotten their start. When he was thirteen years old, he worked helping his father who repaired furniture in the Catskills. They used to go from hotel to hotel asking if there was any furniture to repair. At one hotel the manager wanted a large davenport and chair repaired.

"I'll do it for thirty dollars," the father offered.

"I'll give you one dollar an hour," the man said.

Buddy's father did some fast mental arithmetic. He figured the job would take one day, so a dollar an hour each for him and Buddy would be sixteen dollars. It was less than the job was worth but he needed the money desperately so he agreed.

"He's only a kid," the man said, pointing to Buddy. "Him, I'll give one dollar *a day*."

Buddy's father was in no position to argue. He and Buddy worked hard all day completing the job. Their pay was nine dollars.

Years passed. Buddy became an up-and-coming comedian earning $500 a week. One day a hotel manager came to hire him as an entertainer. Buddy recognized him as the man for whom he and his father had repaired the couch years before and immediately upped his price to $600 a week. The manager, who did not recognize the rotund comedian, promptly agreed. Then Buddy thought about the time he and his father had got only nine dollars for a thirty-dollar job.

"Instead of $600," said Buddy, "I want $621."

He got it, too.

Buddy says his mother was a terrible cook because she made everything too hot. She wasn't so much a cook as an arsonist.

"Her horseradish was so hot it would clear your nasal passages," he recalled. "It was like Jewish Dristan." There was one meat dish, Buddy claims, that was so tough it had to be cooked twenty-four hours. "If you took it off the fire after only twenty-three hours," he says, "you could wear it for a belt."

Buddy acquired chronic heartburn from his mother's fiery cuisine. "When I went in the Army I thought I was dying," he told me. "The fire in my stomach had gone out."

In the Army, Buddy was assigned to the automotive pool. One day he was sleeping under a truck when the phone rang. A voice barked, "Soldier, what vehicles have you got available?"

Buddy reeled off the list. Then, in a moment of whimsey, he added, "We also have Big Butt Johnson's car."

There was a frigid pause. "Soldier, do you know who *this* is? This is Colonel Johnson, and that's no way to talk."

There was another pause. Then Buddy asked, "Do you know who *this* is, Colonel Johnson?"

"No!" snapped the Colonel.

"Well, bye-bye, Big Butt," said Buddy.

Buddy stands five-feet-six, weighs over two hundred pounds and has a voice like a hacksaw. I once asked him if his strange voice was natural. "Do you think I'd talk like this," he demanded, "if I didn't have to?"

Despite his odd manner of speech, Buddy is quick on the

up-take. One night, while leading into a commercial for a flea and tick powder, I asked, "Buddy, have you got a tick?"

"I don't even have a watch," he grumbled.

Another time I was extolling the virtues of Adolph's Meat Tenderizer. "I tried it but I had to give it up," Buddy remarked. "I eat very slowly and it was tenderizing my lips."

At one point Buddy was under contract to Universal-International Studios. "It specified I couldn't make a picture for any other studio," he said. "Then they typed in: 'For us, neither.'"

Buddy was later under contract to 20th Century-Fox. His attractive wife Sherry wasn't happy in Hollywood so he had the studio deduct a hundred a week from his salary and put her under contract for that amount as a starlet. One night he told me on the air how she was enrolled in the studio's dramatic school taking acting, riding and other courses to groom her as an actress.

"The studio heard and got so mad they closed the school," he told me later. "Even though her salary was really coming out of mine, they were spending a fortune on coaching her."

Sherry and Buddy met when he was a young comic in the Catskills. "Her name was Sherine DuBois and it sounded so romantic," Buddy sighed. "Then I met her mother—Esther Cohen."

Sherry is devoted to Buddy and watches over him carefully—especially in regard to drinking. Buddy and I spent one Thanksgiving Day in Hollywood together. We wanted to have a couple of drinks to celebrate the holiday so Buddy called Sherry in New Jersey.

"Not a glassful," she said and Buddy, who is very conscientious, spent the evening drinking out of a vase. We had an uncorking good time.

One day Sherry told Buddy they had to join a Temple. "Why do we have to join a Temple?" he asked.

"So our children will know they're Jewish."

"They know they're Jewish," said Buddy. "They got heart-burn all the time."

As usual Sherry won her point and the Hacketts joined a Temple. A few days later, Buddy told me, a man called up and said that he was Mr. Schine from the Cemetery Committee.

"He wants to show me a burial plot," Buddy said. "I'm thirty-five years old and my wife is twenty-five, and we don't even have a couch yet. He says the members of the congregation think it would be nice if we all spent Eternity together.

"So I said to him, 'Look, Mr. Schine, I don't wanna upset you, but aren't you aware that I don't hang around with you guys too much, even *now?*'"

"Ask Hugh Downs the time," my producer Paul Orr once told me, "and he'll tell you how to make a watch."

It's true.

Hugh knows more about more things than anyone I know. His idea of a big time is sitting home reading a medley of Supreme Court decisions. Just sitting next to him on our panel is Instant Education, and I expect N.B.C. to award me a diploma when my contract is up.

I don't see where he gets time to sop up so much knowledge. He's one of the best and busiest performers on the air. In addition to our show, he has his own show, *Concentration,* seen five times a week in the daytime and once a week at night on N.B.C. Television. He also appears regularly on the *Monitor* radio program, does occasional special shows and performs in summer theater.

However, with Hugh his busy career seems merely a sideline. He has written several fine pieces of serious music, among them the "Elegiac Prelude in A Minor," which was performed by the St. Louis Symphony Orchestra. He is a member of the Citizens Advisory Committee on Mental Hospitals of New York State and a Director of the Manhattan Mental Health Society, as well as belonging to the Royal

Canadian Astronomical Society and the British Interplanetary Society. Hugh has also written a book and recorded an album of folk songs with guitar accompaniment.

Apart from that he just relaxes. Of course his relaxation is rather strenuous. He is an expert skin-diver and, to keep in trim, he gets up at six each morning and jogs a couple of miles around Central Park.

As a result of this strenuous brain-flexing, Hugh is up to his armpits in culture. He knows something about almost anything under the sun and too much about most things.

He once did a science show for young people and a reporter made the mistake of asking him what it was about.

"You see, the postulation that man and nature are separate is outmoded," Hugh said. "Man is now recognized as being a part of nature, and not a power that manipulates nature. Because concepts are always changing, this show does not equate the words truth or final truth with science, but follows Plato's idea that a fact is mortal, an idea immortal."

The reporter went away talking to himself.

However, Hugh's vast assortment of miscellaneous knowledge comes in handy on our program where he can explain almost anything. One night Merv Griffin and his pretty wife were telling about the compost pile on their farm and they referred to it as mulch.

"Mulch is not compost," Hugh corrected. "It's any surface cover that prevents moisture from escaping from the soil. It can be rocks."

"I thought mulch was heavy milk," said Jack E. Leonard.

"No," interjected Charley Weaver. "Rock Mulch is a new western TV star."

Another night I told about having fallen while water skiing, and Hugh gave a long and learned discourse on the intricacies of the sport.

"When you drown, Hugh," I suggested, "you'll know the reason why."

Despite his frightening erudition, and though he seems like the most suave, self-possessed person in the world, I have a revelation to make. Hugh is human. In fact, he has confessed to me that he is occasionally plagued by the same minor crises that haunt us all and that even massive injections of culture have not made him immune to those embarrassing little situations with which our lives seem to be booby-trapped.

One of these occurred in Detroit when he was applying for his first driver's license. The examiner had a brusque manner and began shooting questions at him in a suspicious way. Hugh became increasingly flustered by the man's rude manner. Finally the examiner shoved the application abruptly across the desk and snapped, "Sign your name."

Completely rattled by this time, Hugh went blank and sat staring dumbly at the form. The man glowering at him increased his mental lapse. "That's funny," he finally murmured apologetically. "I know it as well as I know my own name!"

Hugh had a somewhat similar experience in confusion once when he had his tonsils out. It was a simple operation but he remained in the hospital overnight. That evening, while he was dozing, a Catholic priest rushed in. From his haste it was obvious that he was rushing to administer the last rites to some patient and had got in the wrong room.

Startled, Hugh groped for words to tell the priest he was in the wrong room. "Father, I'm here for only a short time," he finally blurted out.

"I know, son," soothed the priest. "That's why I'm here. We're all here for only a short time."

Although Hugh is extremely attractive to women, he is actually very reserved. If he had been a chaperone for Adam and Eve, I'm afraid there would have been no human race. At first our show was a great strain to him because of the informal way we carry on, kissing the lady guests when they come on. Gradually, however, he has adjusted to this wholesale kissing and now busses the female guests with a debonair flourish.

One night we had a succession of glamorous lady guests and Hugh planted a resounding smack on each. Then his wife Ruth came out as a surprise guest, and he shook hands with her with great formality.

Another time Sheila and Gordon MacRae were on the show. They were extremely affectionate, cuddling and nuzzling during the program, and kissing during the commercial breaks.

"Aren't they wonderful?" Hugh whispered. "It makes me so excited watching them that I want to rush home and shake hands with Ruth."

Once Hugh and Ruth went to Washington for a meeting with N.B.C. executives. After the meeting they were scheduled to fly back to New York but the weather turned bad and he decided to take the train.

Ruth was showering, so Hugh called the travel desk of the hotel and asked if they could get them on a train. The desk called back and said they could get them a five o'clock train but it was then ten minutes past four and they would have to hurry to make it. Since Ruth was still in the bathroom, Hugh slammed everything, including her things, into their luggage and called the bellhop who came and got it.

Then Ruth poked her head out of the bathroom, wrapped in a towel, and said, "Dear, would you hand me my green dress?"

The *Concentration* program has offices in Rockefeller Center where they select the contestants for the show. There is a medical laboratory on the same floor and on one occasion a lady who had been sent to the laboratory got into the *Concentration* office by mistake. She said she had come for her test and the receptionist, assuming she meant a program test, gave her a card to fill out.

She was dutifully doing this when she looked up, puzzled, and asked, "Why do you want to know about my hobbies?"

"Oh, that's very important," the receptionist said.

The lady began to get the feeling that something was amiss. "When will my examination be?" she asked.

"Oh, when the others get here," was the reply.

"You mean that others will be tested with me?"

"Oh, yes. Usually about a dozen at a time."

"Perhaps I'm in the wrong place," said the woman, holding up a little bottle.

She was.

One of the quickest men with a quip I know is Joey Bishop, whose sad expression gives him the look of an untipped waiter. In contrast to the new crop of sick comics, Joey's humor is in excellent health.

When Joey first came on our show he had been knocking around in clubs for years without getting anything on fire, including the crepes suzette. In no time at all, it seemed, he was a star, making pictures, joining Frank Sinatra's clan, getting his own TV series and acting as emcee for the $100-a-head inaugural gala for President Kennedy.

"I'm now working in places," he told me, "where a year ago I couldn't afford to go."

Joey has come a long way, and it wasn't easy. He was born Joey Gottlieb in the Bronx and grew up in Philadelphia where his father had a bicycle shop. The father was a strict disciplinarian. "I was belted so much," recalls Joey, "that until I was twelve I thought I was on a dog team."

As a kid he started playing amateur nights with two pals. They called themselves the Bishop Brothers after a Negro boy who drove them around to their engagements.

After World War II Joey struck out on his own playing small night clubs. It was tough going. "Sometimes the crowds were so quiet," he remembers, "I'd suggest we hold hands and try to contact the living. In some places my cuff links were bigger than the dance floor."

Once he had to follow Danny Thomas when that veteran comedian gave a performance that left the audience limp. The shaky Joey knew he could never follow such a smash performance. He ran out on stage, yelled, "That goes for me, too," and kept right on going.

Once he appeared with Frank Sinatra at New York's Copacabana. He came offstage after performing to be met by Frank who asked, "Well, how were they?"

"Great for me," Joey answered. "I don't know how they're going to be for *you*."

With Sinatra boosting him, Joey graduated to the plusher clubs. There he developed his low-pressure but finely honed humor.

Despite his success in nightclubs, Joey was not well-known nationally until the exposure on our show introduced his wry talents to a mass audience. He was an immediate hit.

Joey has a wonderful knack for self-editing. One night he sat for a half-hour on our panel without saying a thing. Finally he raised his hand.

"Yes, Joey?" I inquired.

"Nothing, Jack," he said. "Just wanted you to know I was still here."

Joey is one of the quickest men on the comeback I know. One night we talked about Pavlov's experiments with dogs in Russia. I explained that by ringing bells when they fed the dogs, and then ringing bells and *not* feeding them, the Russians caused the animals so much anxiety they went insane.

"Maybe they weren't trying to drive the dogs nuts," Joey suggested. "Maybe they were just trying to train the bell."

Another night Louis Nye suggested that if Joey wore a toga he would look like Julius Caesar.

"You should see me coming out of a steamroom," Joey said. Then he turned to me and added, "Do *you* think I look like Julius Caesar?"

"You look like a Jewish Caesar," I suggested.

"Et tu, Brute," cracked Joey.

Since his success on television, Joey has his own series and has appeared in a couple of pictures. I asked him the difference between working in TV and nightclubs.

"The big problem in TV," he mused, "is getting used to eating breakfast in the morning."

Joey's idea of a big time is a game of golf with some of his pals and lunch afterwards. He always includes his caddy in the lunch. Someone once pointed out to him that it was rather unusual to invite the caddy to lunch after a round of golf.

"If not for fate," observed Joey, "I'd be carrying the bag and the caddy would be playing golf."

Some of the brightest hours on our midnight talkathon have been provided by the new young Negro comedians like Dick Gregory and Nipsey Russell, who for the first time have brought adult Negro comedy to the American scene. There have been a few Negro comedians in the past, such as Stepin Fetchit, Jack Benny's Rochester and Amos and Andy's King-fish, but they were the old-fashioned, low-comedy colored comics. It has been almost fifty years since the great Negro comedian, Bert Williams, was a big star, and the change in attitude toward the colored entertainer since is illustrated by an incident that once happened to him in Cleveland.

After Williams had entertained with Eddie Cantor, to a tremendous ovation, they went back to their fashionable hotel and Williams had to use the service elevator. As they rode up, Cantor asked the great colored star how it felt to have to ride in the back elevator.

"It wouldn't hurt so much," Williams said, "if I couldn't still hear the applause ringing in my ears."

Although we have come a long way since then, in the matter of breaking down prejudice, and our Negro entertainers are now widely accepted, it was not until the last year or so that a new kind of colored comedian emerged, employing humor as a form of social criticism. Perhaps the best known of these, finding humor in wry commentary on the changing relations between Negroes and whites, is Dick Gregory, a twenty-eight-year-old comic from St. Louis who has recently burst large upon the public consciousness. Dick was working in small nightclubs around Chicago when we heard about him and put him on our show. His acceptance was immediate and overwhelming.

Dick has a gift for discussing real problems like integration but cloaking them in humor and without bitterness. Some sample remarks are:

"I've got a kid brother who was sitting in at a lunch counter. After six months, when they finally integrated, they didn't have what he wanted."

"I wouldn't mind paying my income tax if I knew it was going to a friendly country."

"Baseball is the only sport in the world where a Negro can shake a stick at a white man and not start a riot."

Most of his humor is drawn from his early life in a large and very poor family in St. Louis. "When I was seven," he recalls, "my father went out for a paper. He ain't been back since." He remembers when the public swimming pools were integrated in his home town. "Our parents made everyone go whether they could swim or not. They hired a new lifeguard for us. He was blind. We got up on the diving board and jumped. They'd drained the pool."

Although his family was desperately poor, Dick became a track star and went to college on an athletic scholarship. Once his coach told him, "Take it easy. This is a tough boy you're racing against."

"Don't tell me about *him*," Dick replied. "Go tell him about *me*."

After college he worked in the Chicago post office. "Whenever I'd see a letter postmarked Mississippi," he chuckles, "I'd put it in the sack marked 'Foreign.' " Later he worked in small Negro nightclubs around Chicago for ten dollars a night. He got his first break when a comic at a big nightclub got sick and he was called to substitute.

There was a big convention in town, and many in the audience were Southerners, but he made a big hit. He was supposed to play fifteen minutes but he went on for an hour and a quarter. The Southerners laughed as hard as anyone at his racial sallies.

"Once I was eating in a restaurant and three members of the Ku Klux Klan surrounded me," he said. " 'You can't eat that chicken in here,' they said. 'Whatever you do to that chicken we'll do to you.' So I kissed the chicken."

Dick's comedy is as topical as the morning newspaper, from which he draws much of it. He is a chain smoker and is usually wreathed in smoke even when performing. "I read so much about cigarettes and cancer," he says, "that I finally had to give up reading." Actually, he says, there's a reason for his chain smoking. "Last year," he recalls, "I deducted 10,793 cartons as a business expense. The tax man said, 'Don't *ever* let us catch you without a cigarette in your hand.' "

Despite his amiability, Gregory can squelch a heckler if need be. One night at the *Blue Angel* a ringsider made some slurring remarks.

"You don't have to stay," Dick retorted. "Just finish your drink, burn your cross and leave."

He is delighted with his success because it is opening the doors for other Negro comedians. "We need more Negroes on TV," he told me. "We sit at home and watch Dinah Shore blow the whole world a kiss, and we know it wasn't meant for us."

Dick is now an established star earning around $1,500 a week. After his first appearance on our show, he called his wife to see how she'd liked his TV debut. She hadn't been able to see it. While he was in New York for his appearance, the finance company had repossessed the set.

Another tremendously talented young Negro comedian who made his TV debut with us is Nipsey Russell. Nipsey, who is a college graduate, speaks fluent French and has a vocabulary in English that makes even Hugh Downs blink. Like Dick Gregory he draws most of his comedy from gentle but perceptive observations about racial problems.

"They've been working on a plan to integrate churches in the South," he says. "A delegation went down for that purpose. They contacted the N.A.A.C.P. and asked how long you can legally hold a man under water when you baptize him."

Nipsey feels we are moving toward clearing up the misunderstanding that creates tension between the races in the South. "There is misunderstanding but not antipathy," he says.

I asked him about the problem of Negroes being refused service in some restaurants. He told a story about George Jessel taking a Negro friend to a restaurant. The restaurant said they had no reservation and Jessel said, "Abraham Lincoln made the reservation."

Nipsey's humor is directed as much at Negroes as whites. He told of a colored fan going to see Jackie Robinson in his first big-league game. When Robinson struck out, the frustrated colored man said, "Aw, Joe Louis would have murdered Dempsey."

Louis Lomax, a Negro writer, has also discussed on the show the emergence of the new kind of colored comedian. He believes that it has been brought about by the diminishing of discrimination and the growing pride of the Negro. Negroes have been laughing at their problems in private for years, he said. At home they laughed at *Amos 'n Andy,* but in public they were indignant about it because it represented the old stereotype of the Negro as amusing but servile, lazy and improvident. Louis also was able to see both sides of the problem, and to find humor in it.

He told of a white lady getting on a crowded bus on New York's Madison Avenue and taking the only remaining seat, which was next to a colored lady. The bus gradually began to empty and the white woman decided she would be less crowded if she moved to an empty seat. She realized, however, that to move out of the seat with the colored lady might be interpreted as a slight, so she continued to sit there uncomfortably, ignoring the empty seats.

Finally the colored lady snapped, "There's plenty of room on this bus. Why are you sittin' here crowdin' me?"

12

The Lively Ladies

HUGH DOWNS, who has always seemed to me the epitome of the intellectual aw-shucks type, confessed on our show one night that he once belted his wife in a fit of husbandly pique.

I have never been tempted to belt my wife (oh, maybe tempted a wee bit once or twice) but I have met a few ladies I could cheerfully have slugged upon occasion. It usually has to do with conversation, at which they never seem to run down. I know some women who are such ardent conversationalists that if you gagged them they would talk intravenously.

However, I have in the course of our midnight talkathon met some of the liveliest lady talkers extant. One of the funniest is Peggy Cass, who was once described as a sterling example of the girl you invite just once to a party. After three years of talking up a storm with us, Peggy has now graduated to a situation comedy called *The Hathaways* in which she co-stars with three chimpanzees.

Peggy had some trouble adjusting to a program where her conversational foils are chimpanzees who, in addition, are the world's worst scene-stealers. However, she is handling her co-stars with kid gloves. "I ain't gonna get in no fight with three primates," she said.

Peggy told me she works from seven A.M. to seven P.M. filming the new series. "My grandparents left Ireland because they worked twelve hours a day for some rich guy," she complained. "Now I'm working twelve hours a day for some rich guy. They needn't have made the trip!"

Peggy has come a long way from the jittery young lady

who came on our show three years ago saying she didn't have a thing to say—and then rambling on so vehemently I could scarcely wrest the microphone back. Since then she got an Oscar nomination for the role of the pregnant secretary in *Auntie Mame,* starred on Broadway in *A Thurber Carnival* and now has her own series.

Peggy first got bitten by the acting bug at Cambridge High and Latin School near Boston, where she was in the rooting section. "We all wore the same kinds of sweaters," she recalls, "and we each had a letter on our sweater. I was the 'M' in Cambridge. It was the only letter without a bulge."

After a stint as a secretary, Peggy made her Broadway debut in a review called *Touch and Go.* It wasn't until ten years and ten million words later, however, that she became famous on our show and then on Broadway in *A Thurber Carnival.*

Some of Peggy's excitement at first seeing her name up in lights was dampened by the fact that at the premiere the first letter in Cass was missing. An electrician hurriedly repaired the embarrassing oversight.

Peggy's ego suffered additional damage when she was invited for a weekend at a plush resort in the Catskills. The management sent a limousine to meet her and gave her the most luxurious suite—with flowers, fruit and a magnum of champagne. However, the card read: "Welcome, Peggy Katz."

Peggy's best friend is Jean Kerr, the playwright. In fact, Jean's hit play, *Mary, Mary,* is based partially on Peggy's life. However, when Peggy applied for the feminine lead, her friend told her, "Peggy, you're just not the type."

Peggy was wounded, but not mortally. She and Jean are both Catholics, and the night the hit play opened Peggy sent a wire saying simply: "Hail Mary, Mary."

I once asked Peggy if her husband was older than she is. "Yes, he is," she said, "and he gets more older than I am each year."

During a theatrical strike in New York Peggy and her husband, who is a theatrical manager, found themselves on opposite sides.

"We had a fight," she said, "and he made me sleep on the sofa. He used to greet me each morning by saying, 'Good morning, Nikita.' "

Peggy also said that after the strike five actresses who played nuns in *The Sound of Music* never went back to the show. "They liked the outside world too much," she added.

Peggy tells me that people often stop her on the street to ask what I'm really like.

"I used to tell them that you are a nice, friendly, loyal guy," she said, "but that never seemed to satisfy them. Now I turn on them with blazing eyes and say that you're a no-good bum. That seems to make them feel better. They say, 'I knew it all the time.' "

Another of my favorite lady conversationalists is Hermione Gingold, the British actress, who came to us in a cultural exchange for Benedict Arnold. Hermione has a distinctive way of speaking which was once described as sounding like "asthma set to music." When I first met Hermione I asked her about her first impression of America, as her ship sailed in past the Statue of Liberty. "I liked it," she said, "but I couldn't help but wondah why they had a statue of Judith Anderson in the harbah."

Hermione's name, which is pronounced Her-my-oh-knee, puzzles many Americans. Jack Benny once said to her, "You seldom hear the name Hermione."

"On the contrary," she said, "*I* hear it all the time."

Someone once enthused to Hermione about an actor who spent most of his time on the road, describing his performance as a *tour de force*. "No, no, m'dear," corrected Hermione. "A *force de tour*."

Hermione looks so young that no one suspected her age until she appeared on Ralph Edward's *This Is Your Life*.

"They brought out my sons," she recalled, "and they were older than I was."

I once asked her if her husband was living.

"That," she said, "is a matter of opinion."

When she and her husband were divorced, he was broke and she didn't ask for alimony. Now, however, he is quite well-to-do. Recently she met him at a party.

"Darling, what about alimony?" she asked.

"My dear," he said. "I would never take money from a woman."

Despite her lack of alimony, Hermione once owned a Rolls Royce. She gave it up, she said, because the Rolls Royce people were such snobs.

Once the top of her car was damaged and she took it to the garage. "What do you suggest I do with this roof? Have it covered?" she asked.

"No, Modom," replied the Rolls man. "We suggest you have it thatched."

Hermione confessed to me that she is over sixty. "When I was twenty," she mused, "I said I'd rather die than be an old lady of forty. And when I became forty I felt I could never face life after fifty. But now that I'm sixty, something's happened. I'm rather fascinated by the thought of eventually reaching eighty."

Another rather startling conversationalist is Geneviève, the charming French gamin, whose English pronunciation seems to have retrogressed steadily ever since I've known her. However, I wouldn't change one mangled word of her vocabulary. I've never been a baseball fan but the national pastime seems to take on a certain charm when Geneviève reads me such scores as, "Jawn Fran-zees-ko three, Zeen-zeen-naughty two."

People sometimes complain to me that they have difficulty understanding her but, and this I love, she complains just as vehemently that she can't understand them. When Brendan

Behan, the Irish writer, was on the show, she whispered, "Cheri, I cannot understand eez Eeng-leesh."

The petite French chanteuse has a fierce Gallic temper when aroused—as I discovered during the last Presidential campaign. One night, after Robert Kennedy had been on the program, we all went out to dinner later with Mr. and Mrs. Kennedy and Robert Morley, the English actor.

We were enjoying our food, and Geneviève's fractured English, when a group of raucous men at a nearby table began to make remarks directed at Bobby Kennedy. One of them, who had obviously imbibed too freely, said, "Why don't you go back to summer camp?"

I could see that Bobby, a wiry, tough, ex-Harvard football player, was seething, but since a brawl with a group of drunks would scarcely aid his brother's campaign he sat grimly ignoring the witless insults. Not so Geneviève.

Advancing on the noisy table with eyes burning fiercely she snapped, "Monsieur, you zhut your moof."

They did, too—*tout de suite.*

Science will be pleased to learn that speculation over what would happen if an irresistible force met an immovable object was settled one night on our program. Zsa Zsa Gabor and George Jessel both began talking at once. The outcome, after a heated exchange, was that the irresistible Zsa Zsa flounced off in a high dudgeon.

This is the only time I have ever known the Hungarian beauty to be perturbed by anything, particularly a man, and I have known her for some time. In fact, I know Mama Gabor and all three of her glamorous daughters, which helps to keep my blood circulating briskly.

One night Zsa Zsa came on the show and announced, "Dollink, I haff a terrible hanging-over."

She did too—and not just of the alcoholic variety. One look at her cleavage and I was nearly smitten with skin-blindness.

Zsa Zsa is presently unattached, her third and last husband

having been George Sanders, the actor. Since California has strict community property laws, I once asked her how she and Sanders divided their palatial Bel Air estate when they were divorced.

"It was easy, dollink," she laughed. "I gave him the gate."

Like many beautiful women, Zsa Zsa is mysterious about her age. She once gave herself a birthday party but refused to tell her age on the grounds that it might incriminate her mother.

"You can determine Zsa Zsa's age the way you do a tree," a friend said, "by counting the number of rings."

Zsa Zsa protests, however, that she is not material-minded. One night we were discussing her sister Eva. "Eva has lots of money," Zsa Zsa said, "but I give everything away."

A woman in the audience laughed.

"Not what you think, Madame," Zsa Zsa snapped.

There was a pregnant silence.

"Sometimes I do that, too," added Zsa Zsa.

Perhaps the most unlikely lady to ever become an overnight hit on our show was Selma Diamond, a woman comedy writer from Brooklyn. Selma came on one night with a note pinned to her handkerchief saying, "Watch your language," and became nationally popular by disregarding her own advice.

Selma has red hair, a trim figure, a quick wit and a voice like the *Voice of Firestone*, with the brakes on. She has written for Groucho Marx, Jimmy Durante, Tallulah Bankhead, Milton Berle and Sid Caesar, and now writes for Perry Como.

I once asked her what men think about working with a woman humor-writer. "I'm like Red China," she rasped. "I'm there but they don't recognize me."

Selma got her start in radio, writing for Ed Gardner on *Duffy's Tavern*. Gardner was noted for his large stable of writers and had thirteen of them when Selma was with him.

One day she and Ed walked into a room for a script conference and there were so many writers all the chairs were taken.

"I have noplace to sit," Selma told Gardner.

He pointed to one segment of the small mob of writers and barked, "Everybody on that side of the room is fired."

She now works for Goodman Ace, the head writer of the Como show. One night, after a writing session, she offered to drop Ace off on her way home. Goody mumbled his address but the cabbie didn't get it. Ace repeated it and the driver still didn't understand him.

"I was on the radio for twenty years making my living as an actor," Ace said, sarcastically.

"I know," said the driver, "and I couldn't understand you then, either."

Selma struck a responsive chord on our show talking about her desire to find a husband. "This is how I think of marriage," she said. "You wake up in the middle of the night and you say, 'I want a drink.' At least there's someone there to say, 'You're thirsty—then get up and get a drink.' It's friendly."

She said that after appearing on the show she heard from a great many men. "I've gotten lots of proposals," she said. "One was for marriage. I'm looking into the others, too."

Selma says that people recognize her on the street and come up and call her Selma. "I now have a single name," she says, "like Picasso, Garbo, Drano."

"What's it like now that you're physically known?" I once asked her.

"Physically I'm not known," she complained. "That's my trouble."

Selma says that some men invited her to meet them at Grossinger's, a resort in the Catskills, but that she had been there before with discouraging results.

"I put on a bikini," she said. "When you're offering merchandise the packaging is important. A man offered to teach me how to swim and I remembered to say I didn't know how.

The show from the Friedrichstrasse in Berlin
touched off a national furor in the press.
Being interviewed is Col. Wayne Winder.

We found the Russian people grave but friendly. Here Randy talks to a Russian child near St. Nicholas Cathedral.

In Moscow, Randy and I danced in this magnificent grand ballroom of the former Palace of the Czars.

LOOK Magazine

In Japan
I practice karate—
the art of self-defense.
It comes in handy on our show.

Charley Weaver, the last of the big-time savers,
bargains with us over ice cream cones in Rome.

*In Rome we did as the Romans do
in this visit to the Forum.*

My moment of truth. The truth is I didn't want to fight anything I couldn't milk.

Director Nicholas Ray
coaches Randy for
a part in MGM's
King of Kings
in Madrid.

*If Paul Revere
had ridden one of
these things
we'd still be singing
"God Save the Queen."*

The big question in the 1960 Presidential campaign,
said The New York Times, *was not . . .*

who could stand up to Khrushchev,
but who could sit down with Jack Paar.

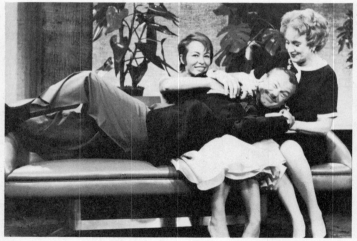

RAYMOND BOREA

*An exercise in group therapy
with Geneviève and Hermione Gingold.*

ON THE JACK PAAR SHOW

RAYMOND BOREA

*Hugh Downs is my faithful Tonto and
our resident intellectual. Ask Hugh
the time and he'll tell you how to make a watch.*

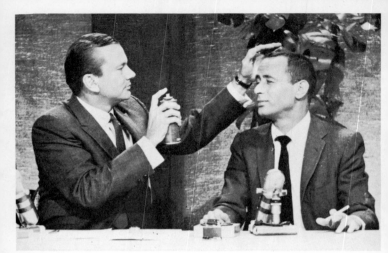

*Joey Bishop looks like
an untipped waiter.*

*Buddy Hackett says our show is
the only place where a Jew
can go to confession.*

*Alex King is the most
exciting man I know,
sitting down.*

*The greatest clown alive today,
in my opinion, is Red Skelton.*

In Berlin Peggy Cass and I
didn't think we were Huntley and Brinkley.
We felt more like Laurel and Hardy.

Then he said, 'I'm so glad you showed up. I was getting so tired of the young ones.' What made me mad was that it was when I was twenty-six. The first time."

One night after the show, Selma was greeted by Miss Miller, the elderly lady who has come to our program nearly every night since it started. "Hello, Selma," said Miss Miller. "I'm a single girl too, you know."

"Yeah," said Selma. "We must double date some night."

Even though she works with men writers, Selma says her job doesn't offer much chance for romance. "Sometimes I'm working with men who are breaking up with their wives," she told me, "but then the show goes off for the summer. The next time I meet them they're remarried. When they're between wives, I'm between shows."

Selma concedes that her failure to get married thus far may be due to her technique. "People say you have to keep men guessing," she said. "I have a married friend who says that even after five years of marriage her husband is still guessing. She has four children and one on the way. So where's the guesswork?"

Selma seems to enjoy her new-found recognition, but she says that it, too, can cause romantic complications. A friend of hers, in the diplomatic service, who had been away in Europe for a long time, returned recently and invited Selma to dinner. People in the restaurant recognized her and kept coming by her table to speak to her and ask for her autograph. Her date seemed confused and finally excused himself. He returned after an interval and Selma asked where he'd been.

"I was so puzzled over all the attention that people are paying you," the man confessed, "that I went out and gave the Men's Room attendant a dollar to tell me who you are."

"So he told you that I get all the attention because of my appearances on *The Jack Paar Show?*" Selma asked.

"Yes," the man said. "Here's another dollar. Now explain who Jack Paar is."

13

Some Great Wits

IT'S AMAZING what they do with conversation these days. They record it on discs and sink it in time capsules. They tape it and send it up in satellites. President Eisenhower even had a conversation with Prime Minister Diefenbaker of Canada that was bounced off the moon!

The only thing that science hasn't mastered yet, unfortunately, is how to make conversation interesting or funny. That still has to be done by the old-fashioned Do-It-Yourself method, and good talk is hard to come by. That's why I've always felt that the greatest fringe benefit of my sometimes precarious calling has been the opportunity to rub elbows and bandy words with some of the greatest wits and conversationalists of our day.

One of them was George S. Kaufman, the brilliant playwright, whose last public appearance was on our show. No one understood better than Mr. Kaufman, who had more than almost anyone, how rare a commodity is wit.

Abe Burrows once called him to ask his advice on whether an escalator would be a funny prop in a show. "It all depends," George replied, "on what you say while you're on the escalator."

I was proud to be able to bring Kaufman back to television after he had been banished in 1952 for remarking on a show during the Christmas season, "Let's make this one program on which no one sings *Silent Night*."

Although this remark was aimed at the commercialism of Christmas, some people interpreted it as irreligious and in the ensuing hue and cry he was dropped from TV. It seemed to me the loss was the public's, and not Kaufman's, as humor is always in short supply.

He was famous for his acid tongue, but his heart was gentle. And his mockery of the ridiculous was all-embracing enough to include a few jibes at himself. He was famous for his shock of unruly hair and used to tell me that he liked being on our show on Wednesdays because that was the day he had his hair done.

When I first met him he passed along to me the advice his father gave him as a young man, "Son, try everything in life but incest and folk-dancing."

George was at his best when he was against something. One night on the show he grumbled about his lawyers. "It sounds a little grand, I know, to say my lawyers in the plural," he said. "I didn't start out that way. I started with one lawyer, but you know what happens. One moves in and pretty soon there are seven, all in the same office. They get together all day long and say to each other, 'What can we postpone next?' The only thing they don't postpone, of course, is their bill, which arrives regularly. You've heard about the man who got the bill from his lawyer which said 'For crossing the street to speak to you and discovering it was not you . . . twelve dollars.' "

Despite his tart tongue and awesome appearance, George was a kindly man who helped many people get started in the theater. Once he was asked to write the introduction to a book, which was sent him in manuscript form. He found it peppered with glaring mistakes in spelling.

"I'm not very good at it myself," he wrote the author, "but the first rule about spelling used to be that there's only one z in *is*."

Kaufman was a firm believer in brevity being the soul of wit. When he felt he had talked long enough on our show he would growl, "Now it's time to get the hell out of here."

A doctor told him once that he'd live to be a hundred.

Kaufman replied that he planned to kill himself at eighty.

"How?" asked the doctor.

"With kindness," George said and smiled.

He died at seventy-one, not long after his last appearance on our show.

One of his most famous plays was *You Can't Take It With You*. Perhaps not, but Mr. Kaufman certainly left a lot of wit behind to remember him by.

One of Kaufman's accomplished collaborators was Moss Hart. I first met Moss when he came on our show to discuss his fine book, *Act One*. "I hope," he said, "that you will talk about my book with the same passion that you do about a deodorant."

He also told me that he had watched an earlier show of mine for months when he was in the hospital. "You hadn't yet refined your style," he observed. "If you had added orange juice you would have had pure vitriol."

Hart claimed that the most successful people he knew were unhappy, and confessed that he was a hypochondriac and plagued by insomnia. He told of taking a trip to London, armed with his usual collection of pills. Feeling keyed up on the night of his arrival, and feeling sure that he would have difficulty sleeping, he took several of his assortment of pills to get to sleep.

He finally fell asleep about ten o'clock and awoke feeling rested and refreshed. He showered, shaved and ordered a hearty breakfast and the morning paper.

When his breakfast arrived, along with the paper, he noticed that it was Tuesday's paper. "You brought me yesterday's paper," he protested. "I wanted this morning's."

"This is today's paper," the waiter said.

"What time is it?" asked the confused Hart.

"It's eleven-thirty Tuesday night," said the waiter. "I wondered why you wanted breakfast."

Hart had slept for only an hour and a half.

One of the wittiest actors I ever met was John Barrymore, whom I encountered briefly when I was a young radio announcer in Cleveland and the "Great Profile" was touring with a play called *My Dear Children*.

It was a cold wet day when Barrymore arrived at the railway station. I apologized for our local weather and he grunted an unprintable reply. He was drinking heavily in those days, and was only a shell of one of the greatest actors ever to grace the American stage, yet he still displayed flashes of his old charm and wit.

Later I was in Hollywood during his last sad years when he was playing what amounted to a burlesque of himself.

Garson Kanin told me of directing a picture in which they used a prompting blackboard—the forerunner of TV's "idiot cards" of today—because Barrymore's memory was fading and he couldn't remember his lines.

One day Kanin had the blackboard removed because the set was cramped for space. Soon he heard a loud verbal explosion and found that Barrymore was vigorously protesting the removal, though there was only a single word on it—yes. Barrymore was playing a character named Gregory Vance and the scene required him only to answer the question—"Are you Gregory Vance?"

"Why do you need the blackboard?" Kanin demanded. "What could you say but yes?"

"I could say no," growled Barrymore. "Then where in the hell would you be?"

A friend who was with Barrymore at his death told me his last words. As the once handsome, romantic actor lay dying, an elderly and homely nurse bent over to minister to him.

"Ah, well," Barrymore sighed, looking up. "Jump in anyway."

Two of my favorite comedians, and two of the most delightful, witty guests we ever had on our program, are Jack Benny and George Burns. I link them here because they have been friends almost all their lives and when either one came on the show he spent most of the time talking about the other— a rare thing in actors.

I first met Jack Benny in a hospital on Guadalcanal during World War II, and in 1947 he gave me the break of my life by choosing me as his summer replacement for his radio show —then the most popular program on the air. It was through him that I met George Burns, whom I had long admired. Even before I met Benny I looked up to him as one of the greatest comedians of our generation, and my respect for his talent and for him as a man has grown and deepened over the years.

Both he and George Burns are wonderful raconteurs and I love to hear them reminisce about the great days of vaudeville, when they were young men just starting out in show business.

George Burns and Gracie Allen have been married thirty-six years, a year longer than Jack Benny and Mary Livingston. George and Gracie were married in Cleveland. Benny, who was playing a vaudeville theatre in Kansas City, wired Burns that he would call him that evening to congratulate him and greet the bride.

When Burns picked up the phone, Benny, bursting with sentiment and goodwill, said, "Hello!"

"Send up two hamburgers and coffee," Burns barked, then hung up.

The following year Benny married Mary Livingston, who was only nineteen. The Bennys were married in Chicago and all the way to New York, where they were to meet George and Gracie, Jack fretted about introducing his young bride to Burns, because of his penchant for practical jokes, often quite risqué.

When they finally met, Benny said, "George, this is my wife."

In telling the story on our program, Benny paused at this point.

"What did George say then?" I asked, anxiously.

"Well," smiled Benny. "Your show isn't on late enough for me to tell you."

Although Burns takes a perverse delight in needling Benny, Jack thinks he is the funniest man in the world and practically falls down laughing if George so much as says hello. This has been going on ever since they first knew each other.

In those days, they shared an agent named Tom Fitzpatrick. Fitzpatrick was a tender-hearted man who, whenever he was unable to get an actor a booking, would start rummaging through his desk drawers instead of breaking the bad news.

One day Burns ran into Benny outside the Palace Theater building. "I've just been to see Fitzpatrick," he sighed, "and he gave me the desk drawer routine."

At this, Benny laughed so hard that a crowd gathered on the sidewalk. To escape the mob, they both retreated into a shoe store.

"As long as we're here," Burns suggested, "let's buy a pair of shoes so it won't be a total loss."

That really broke Benny up.

Another time, when George and Gracie Allen were playing the Palace, they encountered a problem over a joke. Joe Frisco had given them the joke—about the bird that flew backwards because it didn't care where it was going—it was only interested in where it had been.

The joke was getting big laughs but Fred Allen told them that he had originated it. They offered him five hundred dollars but Allen refused to part with the joke. Looking for a new one to replace Allen's quip, Burns called John P. Medbury, a newspaper writer and humorist, and explained the problem.

"That's simple," said Medbury. "Switch it so that the bird is flying upside down and explain that it flies that way so if it is shot by a hunter it will fall up instead of down."

Jack Benny once had a similar experience trying to get a good line on short notice.

One night, just before his radio show, he was told that at the end of the program they had to say, "Dennis Day appeared tonight through the courtesy of R.K.O. Pictures."

Nervously, Jack called in his four writers. "We have to find a way," he explained, "to say 'Dennis Day appeared tonight through the courtesy of R.K.O. Pictures.' "

As the time ticked away there was much frenzied discussion on how best to phrase the line. Finally, one of the writers said, "Why don't we just *say* that Dennis Day appeared through the courtesy of R.K.O. Pictures?"

Hastily Benny scribbled in the line that way. As the four writers trooped out, one of them said, "Jack, *two* of us could have handled that."

Burns first started needling Benny when they met and he's still at it after all these years. In vaudeville days, Benny once sent George a funny telegram. He toiled over it painstakingly and felt that the result was hilarious. He dispatched it to Burns who wired back, "Don't worry. I won't show your wire to anyone."

Recently, Benny went to London and was surprised to find how popular the Burns and Allen filmed series was on British television. Touched, he sat down and wrote his old friend a long, sincere and sentimental letter, telling him how pleased he was to see his TV show so popular in England.

Burns cabled back, "Your letter was a scream."

The greatest clown alive today, in my opinion, is Red Skelton. Groucho Marx hails Skelton as the successor to the mantle of Chaplin, and I heartily second the motion.

I once spent a vacation in Las Vegas with Red, when he was appearing there, and it is hard to say which was the greater revelation.

Las Vegas is a sagebrush Babylon in the Nevada desert

which glitters like a mirage seen through the eyes of Zsa Zsa Gabor. Buddy Hackett told me that he got into a taxi there and when the driver threw his flag it came up three cherries.

Buddy had to pay him ten quarters.

There are a half-dozen hotels with extravagant acts and the people wander aimlessly from hotel to hotel, gambling and ogling the entertainment in a trancelike state.

In one place I heard a jaded husband, who had already taken in several shows, ask his wife, "What'll we do now?"

"Go to bed," sighed the weary lady.

"Who's playing there?" asked the husband.

Skelton's wild, inventive and knockabout comedy was a tremendous hit in Las Vegas, despite the distractions of gambling, drinking, and bare-bosomed beauties. Yet although he is a superbly gifted performer who completely captures his audience, Red is an emotional shambles before he goes on, cringing backstage like a man bound for the electric chair. Then, he bounces out—gay, rowdy and mischievous. The finish of his act, in which he plays an old man watching a parade go by, is perhaps the most moving moment I have seen on any stage.

One night while I was in the audience, Red received word that a group of United Arab Republic diplomats were in the audience. He introduced them for a bow before the predominantly Jewish audience. Then, as they stood up, he roared, "Ready! Aim! Fire!"

Sitting with him, he told me about his early days as a young comedian. He used to work on a percentage basis and did his own wrangling with theater managers over terms. Once a manager offered him a slightly higher percentage than usual if he would do his own advertising and Red agreed.

A few days before his scheduled arrival, signs blossomed outside the theater—"HE IS COMING!"

Then, the day of his arrival in the town, new signs went up proclaiming—"HE IS HERE!"

The night of his performance, the theater was jammed

with the curious, attracted by the mysterious ads. The curtains parted, revealing a sign which read—"HE JUST LEFT!"

Red then sauntered out and said, "Well, so long as *he's* not here . . ." and went into his act.

Another versatile performer is Jackie Gleason, whose talent seems to be as great as his gargantuan appetite for living, or his good-natured appreciation of himself. Jackie is a gifted actor, a highly creative comedian, a composer, a prodigious trencherman and tosspot and a wonderful conversationalist and wit.

Recently he combined all of his assorted talents in a motion picture he made in Paris. Although he played the role of a lovable deaf-mute bum, Jackie lived in a style not seen in France since Marie Antoinette. He ensconced himself in the luxurious penthouse of the George V Hotel, toured around in a burgundy and opal Rolls Royce limousine with bar, telephone, refrigerator, TV, stereo hi-fi, and air-conditioning.

In a nation which prides itself on its superb cuisine and fine wines, Gleason stunned the French with the extent of his appreciation. He managed to toss off about six bottles of wine per day, along with champagne, pernod and brandy. Despite his Homeric drinking feats, Jackie posted this sign on the set where they were shooting the picture:

Nobody minds a man having a morning eye-opener and it's OK to have a bracer around ten A.M., and a couple of drinks before lunch. Or a few beers on a hot afternoon, to keep a man healthy or at least happy. And, of course, everyone drinks at the cocktail hour. Nor can a man be criticized for having wine with his dinner, a liqueur afterwards and a highball or two during the evening—but this damn business of *SIP, SIP, SIP* all day long *HAS GOT TO STOP*.

Thinking to capture this new filming technique for history, I wrote Jackie for permission to shoot some film of him in

Paris for our show. He replied that his C.B.S. contract prevented him from doing this. However, he generously added, "You have my permission to do two or three hours of raves about my talent."

This communique was modestly signed: "The Great One."

Jackie was no stranger to tippling, to put it mildly, even before his Paris sojourn. He used to go on monumental eating and drinking bouts and then go into a hospital to recover. The hospital was a fancy one in New York, favored by wealthy people for dieting, rest and hangover cures.

One time when Jackie was in for the usual reasons, a group of his pals came to visit and found his room empty.

"He got sick," a nurse explained, "and we had to send him home."

Jackie sometimes sought solace from the travail of television in drink. This fine actor and comedian once found himself somehow tangled up in a gimmicky panel show that had a disastrous debut. The next week Jackie sent the panel home, disregarded the format, and just talked to the audience for a half-hour.

"I'm telling you, friends," he said, "that I've seen bombs in my day but this one makes the H-bomb look like a two-inch firecracker. I knew the show was bad when I went back to the hotel, looked out the window to see if it was still snowing, and they had the nets up."

While he talked, Jackie sipped from a cup of what he said was a new brand of coffee—Chock Full O' Booze. Actually the beverage was wine.

He said that Arthur Godfrey had tried it when they did a show together. "Afterward we had to carry Godfrey to the car," he said. "The last I heard he was up on the Empire State Building trying to repair the antenna."

Another of the great wits I was fortunate enough to know was the late Fred Allen. During World War II, when Allen

was at the height of his fame on radio, I used to write him
from the jungles of the South Pacific and he would answer
with letters of advice about comedy. Later I met him at a
party in New York.

"Mr. Allen, you've always been my god," I blurted.

"What a shame," Fred cracked. "Five hundred churches in
New York and you're an atheist."

Many of Allen's amusing sallies are well known from his
books and programs, but the ones I like best are the lesser-
known stories that grew out of his reaction to some real
situation.

On one such occasion, he attended a movie preview in a
New York office building. At the end of the film, most of
the audience tried to crowd into the elevators at the same
time. Fred found himself squeezed in along with a stout
woman, just before the door was shut.

"My husband!" screamed the woman. "You've left him outside! You can't go without him!"

"Courage, Madame," Fred said, tapping her on the shoulder.
"This elevator may be going down but it's not the *Titanic*."

14

Fairies and Communists

THERE USED to be a time when it looked like the Communists were taking over show business. Now it's fairies. They operate a lot alike, actually; both have a tendency to colonize. Just as there used to be no such thing as one Communist in a play or a movie, now there is no such thing as one fairy. Where you find one, you usually find a baker's dozen swishing around.

I had a little game I used to play when I was an actor in Hollywood, back in the days when Communists or Communist sympathizers were nearly as plentiful in the film capital as yes-men. If I spotted someone in a picture who was a Communist or leftist, I could usually pick out several others. They always came in sets.

Now I play it a different way. When I hear that some fairy is producing or directing or acting in a play, I can often name some of the rest of the cast, even if I've never heard it.

But Communists and fairies do differ in some respects. The Hollywood Communists had their "Unfriendly Ten," who refused to testify before a Congressional Committee, but the fairies are *over*friendly. They do say no occasionally.

"When a fairy says no," Alex King has observed, "he almost throws his back out of joint."

The poor darlings, as they sometimes call themselves, are everywhere in show business. The theater is infested with them and it's beginning to show the effects. "The New York theater is dying," the late Ernie Kovacs complained recently. "Killed by limp wrists."

The dance is a mecca for the gamboling third sex, which prompted Oscar Levant to observe that "ballet is the fairies' baseball." The movies have long been a happy hunting ground for them, and now they're starting to take over television. No TV variety show seems complete without a group of fairy dancers leaping about with balloons.

George Jean Nathan wrote long ago, "What we need is more actors like Jack Dempsey. Jack may not be much of an actor but his worst enemy cannot accuse him of belonging to the court of Titania." Alas, things have been getting worse ever since.

The increasing emasculation of our stage seems to stem in part from the influence of actors from England, where homosexuality is rampant in the theater. Kenneth Tynan, the British critic, has acknowledged the growth there of the theatrical phenomenon known as "camp" whose distinguishing feature, he says, is a marked inclination toward the dainty, the coy and the exuberantly fussy.

"High comedy in England is nowadays a hostage in the camp of camp," he lamented. "With each new season its voice gets shriller and its blood runs thinner."

Formerly playwrights were writing plays about fairies and now they're writing plays *for* them. There was a wonderful scene in *Peter Pan* when Mary Martin turned and asked the audience if they believed in fairies and they answered with an affirmative roar. I began to get worried when the cast started drowning out the audience.

Not only have homosexuals taken over a leading role in the theater, but the theme of homosexuality is becoming increasingly prominent on the stage as witness *Advise and Consent, Compulsion, The Best Man* and *Tea and Sympathy,* some of which have been produced on both the stage and screen. Recently, not one but two versions of the life of Oscar Wilde were showing in New York.

A half century ago Wilde was jailed and disgraced in England for "the love that dares not speak its name," yet today actors found guilty of the same offense become not only famous but honored. One of England's most noted actors and a popular American male singer have both been convicted of homosexuality without it adversely affecting their public lives or careers.

I first noticed the widespread prevalence of homosexuality in Hollywood, which boasted a Fairyland long before it had a Disneyland. Fresh out of the Army, and rather naïve, it came as quite a shock to discover that some of Hollywood's biggest he-man stars were actually more interested in each other than in the glamorous actresses they made love to before the cameras. One virile looking Western star was such a gay Caballero that he had to be restrained from riding side saddle. Another gorgeous hunk of man, whom millions of girls sighed over, had his voice dubbed by another actor to disguise its girlish quality. Other male stars, known as AC-DC types, are ambidextrous and can't decide what to do when confronted by "His" and "Hers" towels.

In New York they are prominent in all of the arts. They cavort in ballet. They flutter on the Broadway stage. And they are everywhere in television. Wherever there is one you will find others. They are highly organized and indefatigable at assisting each other.

Although fairies are usually cool toward women, for some reason they seem irresistibly attracted to comediennes. Perhaps being a comedienne is unnatural for a woman, like playing the bass fiddle or pole-vaulting, which may be the reason why they have such an attraction for the limp-wristed set. There always seems something terribly sad about many comediennes, for all their talent, as they are almost inevitably surrounded by these demimales.

I once mentioned one such famous comedienne to a friend of mine. "She is terribly amusing," the friend said. Then he added, wistfully: "Of course, she has no alternative."

Once Wilson Mizner, the noted wit, was having lunch at a New York hotel with Marshall Neilan, the director. At an adjoining table were several fairies, giggling as gaily as four suburban housewives having butterscotch sundaes at Schraffts. Annoyed by the girlish carrying-on, Mizner began directing audible disparaging remarks at the group. The giggling died away and the group began to direct some cold glares at Mizner and Neilan. Still Mizner continued to aim his loud barbs until violence seemed imminent.

Neilan suddenly became philosophical. "Wouldn't it be strange," he mused, "if on Judgment Day it turned out they were right?"

I feel quite sure it won't—but that's their problem. I just wish they would leave show business alone, and stop leaping about with their balloons on television.

We occasionally have fashion shows on our program so I've had a chance to observe at firsthand the havoc that limp-wristed designers and hair dressers and make-up men have wrought upon once beautiful girls. When they finish accentuating the hollow cheeks, the pallor and the blue circles under the eyes, the models look less made-up than embalmed.

One night a group of them trooped out modeling bathing suits and they were so skinny and unfeminine I thought it was the mile relay team from the Y.M.C.A. Gradually I've become so accustomed to seeing these bony, boyish figures that I was pleasantly surprised one night when one model appeared displaying a full-blown figure with ample curves. Later I commented backstage on how rare it was now to see a model with curves.

Our wardrobe lady chuckled cynically. "When she took off that bathing suit and dropped it on the floor," she said, "it bounced for five minutes."

Another lovely girl who managed to escape the ministrations of the fairy Svengalis is the 1961 Miss Universe, Marlene Schmidt. She is a tall, ravishing blonde with a figure like God intended women to have, without alterations by Slenderella or some delicate designer. I asked her measurements and she told me they were 95-45-95!

This was in centimeters, it turned out, but even measured in inches her endowments were opulent. The reason she still possessed her naturally lovely figure and rosy-cheeked, healthy face, I discovered, was that she was a recent refugee from East Germany and our fairy fashion fraternity hadn't gotten their clutches on her yet.

Because of all this I've started my campaign to save our starving models by sending them CARE packages. For Christmas I plan to send my friends cards with notes saying that donations in their names have been made to Jinx Falkenburg.

I hope that all red-blooded men will rally to my crusade to have girls look like girls again. If we show our determination I'm sure that women will throw off the tyranny of fairy designers. They have nothing to lose but their falsies.

Meantime, I must go now and give a blood transfusion to Suzy Parker.

15

Vice Presidents I Have Known

ALTHOUGH the United States manages to get along on only one, the J. Walter Thompson advertising agency had one hundred and thirty-two vice presidents the last time I counted. That would seem to be more than enough, yet it is not at all unusual in the communications and allied fields, where executives seem to come only in large groups. There's something about our business that seems to spawn more chiefs than Indians.

The National Broadcasting Company, where I currently toil, has about forty vice presidents. (I say "about" forty because the number changes rapidly.) Practically everyone you meet in the halls of any network is a vice president in charge of something.

There is even an elevator operator at C.B.S. who, catching the fever, describes himself as "vice president in charge of vertical access and egress to all offices, Eastern Division."

This plethora of executives is one of the occupational hazards of the entertainer in the world of business, and many of my performing brethren have difficulty adjusting to the mores of the executive echelon. The late Fred Allen for years carried on a vendetta against N.B.C. vice presidents and advertising executives whom he described as "molehill men."

"A molehill man," he once told me, "is a pseudo-busy executive who comes to work at nine A.M. and finds a molehill on his desk. He has until five P.M. to make this molehill into a mountain. An accomplished molehill man will often have his mountain finished even before lunch."

Fred Allen's ire against network executives began when one of them cut his program off when it ran over. He got cut so often, in fact, that he protested that the last page of his script resembled a Band-Aid. In protest, Fred rounded up some midgets to picket the N.B.C. building with signs reading: "This Network Is Unfair to the Little Man."

I encountered the same trouble in 1960 when an N.B.C. censor snipped a joke about a water closet out of my show without telling me, and I walked off in a huff. However, on this occasion I found my bosses, Board Chairman Robert Sarnoff and President Robert Kintner, more than understanding. They not only sympathized with me but soothed my wounded feelings by dispatching me on a trip to Hong Kong.

Although I have had an occasional scuffle with network brass over the years, my feelings about them are tempered with understanding. They lead a difficult life, fraught with insecurity.

Groucho Marx has noted the uncertain tenure of network executives. When his long-running TV quiz show was cancelled, Groucho observed cheerfully, "I have no complaint. I've gone through two wives and four or five N.B.C. presidents with this show."

Like any field where the rewards are sizable, considerable in-fighting goes on for the top-dog positions and the network top brass have a tendency to form cliques in their struggle for supremacy, or just plain survival. On one occasion the president of N.B.C. called his squabbling factions together and delivered a harangue on the necessity for greater coöperation.

"We must coöperate more closely," he admonished. "We must all pull together. Remember we're all part of the same big team. So let's have no more talk of cliques."

As the chastened executives shuffled out of the meeting,

Mike Dann, a young vice president, remarked *sotto voce,* "The three-thirty meeting of the Mike Dann clique has just been called off."

Some of the network executives I have encountered lead a hectic life, teeming with frustrations and emergencies, while others seem to create their own instant travail. They are really grown-up Boy Scouts, who can build a panic by rubbing two crises together.

In contrast with the furious way in which most network executives go about their chores, a few seem to waft dreamily through the troubled network air. The only noticeable role they fill is, as Yogi Berra once said admiringly of a rival player, "an important clog in their machine."

When I was shuttling between networks in Hollywood, there was one executive who was creating a greater atmosphere of mystery than Alfred Hitchcock. Nobody could figure out what he did. He was installed in a plush office but had no apparent duties. He seemed to spend most of his time gazing out his office window which looked over the Hollywood hills. There was constant speculation among his friends as to what he was supposed to be doing.

One day a group of us were pondering over this, as usual.

"He watches the pass in those hills," John Nelson, an N.B.C. executive, finally suggested, "and if a glacier starts coming through, his job is to warn us."

Although network executives wield vast power, and can make multi-million dollar deals at the drop of a rating, they labor without the recognition accorded royalty. This relative anonymity was demonstrated on one occasion when Allen Funt, the *Candid Camera* snooper, conducted a survey among a group of New York cab drivers as to who would make the best TV czar—one of the three network presidents or J. Fred Muggs, the chimpanzee who occasionally appears on television.

Funt naturally didn't identify Muggs as a chimp, but phrased his question this way: "Who do you think would make the best TV czar—Kintner (president of N.B.C.), Stanton (C.B.S.), Treyz (A.B.C.) or Muggs (chimpanzee)?"

Most of the cabbies, with typical outspokenness, felt that Muggs would make the best executive.

"His name rings a bell with me," one driver observed. "I think he'd clean up whatever needs to be cleaned up."

Another driver said that Muggs sounded like the most dependable of the lot. "I think he'd do a good job," he asserted. "He's a good administrator. I never heard nothing bad about him."

Although it is popular to scoff at advertising men, I admit to an admiration for the anonymous advertising man who first figured out how to get a thirty-eight-inch bust on a nineteen-inch screen.

One of the first real living, breathing, advertising geniuses I ever met was Hubbell Robinson, Jr., an agency executive who stumbled across me (I had my foot out) shortly after my discharge from the Army at the end of World War II. He launched me in network radio as a summer replacement for Jack Benny but, after this original burst of inspiration, Hubbell's judgment seemed to suffer. I made other less successful attempts to get him to hire me later.

While serving as a vice president of C.B.S. in New York, Hubbell developed a disconcerting habit of swiveling his chair around and staring silently out the window while someone expounded a program idea to him.

Once two comedy-writer friends of mine invaded Robinson's C.B.S. sanctum and gave him a rousing description of a program they had dreamed up. Throughout their enthusiastic exposition of the show's merits, Robinson gazed pensively out the window, with his back to them, occasionally grunting a comment.

After the writers left his office, with only a noncommittal grunt about their idea, one of them began fulminating about their treatment. "He might at least have looked at us. All he did was stare out that damned window."

"There was a reason for that," the other writer answered. "He was reading his grunts off cue cards out there."

Another time Orson Welles, the portly self-confessed genius, descended on Robinson with the pilot film of an elaborate series he had just conceived. After the film was shown, Welles waited imperiously for Robinson's comment on it.

"It's great," Hubbell enthused, "but do you think the average guy will understand it?"

"Well," harrumphed Welles, "*you* understood it."

One of the kindest men I ever met in the broadcasting business was Manie Sacks, a homely little sliver of a man with a very large heart. Manie was a top executive at R.C.A. when he died in 1959, and show business hasn't found anyone quite like him.

Once General David Sarnoff, then head of N.B.C., said in a discussion, "Anyone can be replaced." Then he thought for a minute and added, "Except maybe Manie."

Everyone liked Manie, because he liked everyone. He had no former friends. Manie used to negotiate million-dollar deals, yet he was diffident and friendly and never too busy to listen to any actor's problems. He was generous with his time and so generous with his money that they called him "the fastest wallet at Toots Shor's." Manie's secret was that he liked to help people—whether they were big stars or just someone trying to get his foot in the door of show business.

Once when he was flying to Hollywood with Milton Berle, the comedian remarked gloomily that he had forgotten to take out life insurance to cover the flight.

"Take half of mine," Manie said, cheerfully, and endorsed half his policy over to Berle.

When Eddie Fisher was an unknown, struggling to get a break, he used to sleep on the couch in Manie's small apartment.

One day Manie rushed up to the young singer. "Eddie," he exclaimed, "I've found a song that only you can record. Not Como, not Sinatra, not Lanza—only you!"

"Really?" asked the stunned youngster. "Are you serious?"

"Yes," said Manie. "I've been to Como, Sinatra and Lanza, and you're the only one left!"

Manie was known as the man who couldn't say no. In a business famed for shin-kicking and elbowing, Manie couldn't bear to hurt a soul.

One night he was having dinner with a young actress who wanted his advice on her career. Having work to do later, but not wishing to seem to give her the brush-off, Manie told her he had to fly to Chicago later in the evening.

As they left the restaurant, he said good-by but the young actress insisted that she accompany him to his apartment and help him pack. Manie had no recourse but to go to his apartment and pack. He thanked her and once more said good-by. But the young lady insisted on accompanying him to the airport. Manie protested but to no avail, so together they took a cab to the airport, where she waved a cheery good-by as Manie boarded a plane for Chicago. When he got there, he boarded another plane and flew back to New York.

I was at N.B.C. when Manie was taken to the hospital seriously ill. The nature of his illness was not disclosed. But even in the hospital Manie continued to be of assistance to others.

Danny Thomas, an old friend, asked Manie's help in raising money for victims of leukemia. As always, Manie helped— from his hospital bed.

Not long afterwards he died. Of leukemia.

One of the most imposing network executives I ever encountered was Pat Weaver, formerly president of N.B.C., and now a top advertising agency executive. Pat, a lanky, handsome man, with prominent ears and freckles, fathered the *Tonight* show, which I presently adorn, as well as the early morning *Today* show on N.B.C.

Before he joined the exalted ranks of executives, Pat had been a radio comedian himself, and had also served as producer of the Fred Allen show on radio. Although Fred hated network executives, he and Pat were good friends. Their friendship was tested only when Weaver would submit jokes or sketches for the program.

"He submitted one sketch about the Foreign Legion," Fred once grumbled. "I suggested he join it."

Pat has a brother, "Doodles" Weaver, who for a time had a flourishing career as a comic. During Pat's tenure as head of N.B.C., "Doodles" turned up as a comedian on the network. However, Goodman Ace derailed both the show and "Doodles" with a two-word review—"Oh, brother!"

Pat, who often greeted visitors balancing on a Bongo Board, thought only in large terms, and I had difficulty in getting him to think small enough for a mere show for me.

"Every man will walk the craters of the moon," he predicted of TV viewing, "look into the churning lava of Vesuvius, sit in the ruins of Magna Lepta, be present at tribal dances, and range down the corridors of Antland."

While viewers waited for the day when they could walk the craters of the moon, or range down the corridors of Antland, I was hoping they would settle for me. I expressed this modest hope to Pat but he was absorbed in thinking big about a project he called "Operation Frontal Lobes."

To make matters worse, not only did Pat think in global terms but had as an adviser Billy Rose, a man whose feverish imagination envisioned only spectacles involving elephants, or extravaganzas awash with hundreds of splashing mermaids. In desperation, I sent Pat my idea and wired him:

"I hope that Billy Rose and you like my idea. Mr. Rose

may not at first as it's an above sea-level idea, but I'm willing to use an elephant if we can get one for union scale. If you don't like my idea, it's only fair to tell you that a station in Phoenix does."

My idea, alas, never penetrated Pat's roseate visions of TV's future, and Billy Rose went on brooding happily about elephants and mermaids. Despite this cool reception, I have always admired Pat Weaver. He was one of the most creative executives in television, and I have been awed and baffled by his mastery of those twin weapons—the meeting and the memo.

The memo and the meeting are the two prime gambits of the executive echelon in broadcasting, and I have studiously tried to avoid them both. But it was inevitable that I get tangled up in a few while rattling around amid the networks.

Pat's conversational style was a particularly deadly executive weapon, since no one understood it. His small talk was larded with such phrases as "a fortuitous concatenation of circumstances," "contiguity discounts," "the pluralistic nature of twentieth-century cultures," "earing the ground," and "cybernetic civilization."

All this sounded wonderful while Pat was expounding it, and it wasn't until you had left him, teetering precariously on his Bongo Board with arms outstretched like a crane about to take flight, that you realized you hadn't understood a word he said.

Weaver's memos, likewise, were masterpieces of tangled syntax.

"Between Marathon and today," he once wrote, "if you're used to thinking in terms of galactic clusters, which to me immediately sets you aside as somebody that is moving toward mutancy, there isn't much change."

It was little thoughts like that that kept the N.B.C. interoffice phones busy after a meeting with Pat as executives feverishly called each other to ask, "What did he say?"

Pat is an honored pioneer in the obfuscating language of broadcasting and advertising, but he has many a follower treading his footsteps through the jungle of lush verbiage. A recent report proposed by the Young and Rubicam agency bore the awesome title "Reexploration Narrative Interviews to Uncover Conscious and Latent Consumer Needs, Wants and Desires in the Grilled Sandwich Area."

16

Stories in Their Anecdotage

THEY say that nature abhors a vacuum, and there is one vacuum that I'm getting to abhor, too. It's that hour and three-quarters of empty midnight air that I have to fill with something five times a week.

When I took over the *Tonight* show I knew we couldn't depend on written material. Even if it were possible to write that much, which it isn't, there would be no way for the cast to learn lines since we have no rehearsal. I couldn't possibly memorize such great chunks myself and I vetoed as too expensive the suggestion I have the whole script tattooed on the back of my eyelids.

My hunch turned out to be well-grounded. Even with writers, the most I can use is an opening monologue of perhaps ten minutes per night. The remaining hour and thirty-five minutes we just wing it.

We have grappled with the problem in two ways. One was to get talented conversationalists who could ad-lib amusingly and almost endlessly. The other was to take our material where we could find it, to keep a perceptive eye out for the funny things that just happen in the world around us.

Happily, friends and viewers have inundated the show with stories, jokes and anecdotes. I have always preferred the true amusing anecdote to the contrived joke, and some of the biggest laughs I have gotten on the program have been when I told some funny little thing that actually happened to me, to a friend of mine or to some viewer who wrote in. However, I've been tripped up a few times by supposedly true stories that keep coming back as regularly as the swallows to Capistrano.

One day a friend of mine told me a story which he said had happened in Florida and which he swore was true. The driver of a concrete-mixing truck, he said, suspected that his wife was cheating with his boss. One day, while driving his truck, he went by his house to check up. Sure enough, there was the boss's car in his driveway. Infuriated, the truck driver dumped his load of wet concrete over the Cadillac, leaving it half-buried in the hardening cement.

I told the story on the show and got a big laugh. But the laugh, it seemed, was on me. People began to write and call saying that the story was true, all right, but that I had the facts wrong. It wasn't Florida, one would protest, but Wisconsin. Another would say it wasn't a Cadillac, but a Pontiac. I tried to check back on the story, but the details kept changing the further I checked. I finally gave up because of the maze of conflicting reports.

Others tried to track down the elusive cement-buried car, but with an equal lack of success. Pierre Berton, a Canadian newspaper columnist, made a project of trying to track the story back to its source. He finally labeled the story a myth, which only served to antagonize many of his readers. Some wrote in giving actual names and addresses of the parties involved. But the names and addresses were always non-existent.

The story traveled so fast and wide that it had repercussions all over the country. A New York contractor, who owned a Cadillac, put it on public display to prove he wasn't the one involved. A contracting firm in Pennsylvania took ads to say that its employees were all happy with the boss, and vice versa. One New York contractor took an ad which said simply, "It wasn't us."

Bob Sylvester, another columnist, also did some sleuthing on the tall tale. He reported that dozens of people claimed to know the fellow it had happened to. He even got three different photographs of cars with their back seats full of hardened concrete.

He tracked them down and found that in each case some-one thought the story was so funny that he had bought an old car in a junkyard, filled the back seat with cement, and photographed it, just for laughs.

Even now people still tell me they know the man it happened to. The next person who tells me the story, I think I'll bury *him* in concrete.

Pierre Berton, the Canadian columnist who tried to track down the story, says that at least it is a new story and not one of the hoary legends that keep coming back year after year in various reincarnations. Berton was aided in his literary gumshoe work by Gerry Anglin of *Maclean's Magazine,* who has been keeping tabs on such stories for years. Anglin says that the most hardy perennial of all is this story, which he first heard thirty years ago and which still keeps bobbing up periodically.

A housewife, according to the sturdy legend, was planning a bridge party and decided to serve mushroom patties. She cooked the mushroom filling separately and set it out on the back porch. When she checked it a few minutes later, she was horrified to discover that the family dog had been sampling it. The guests were due any minute and there was no chance to prepare anything else. Quickly she ladled the rest of the filling into the patties.

All went well and the guests complimented her on the delicious lunch. However, as they were leaving, and the hostess accompanied them to the door, she was stunned to find their dog lying dead on the porch!

She was faced with a terrible dilemma. Should she admit she'd served her guests a dish the dog had gotten into, or take a chance on their dying of mushroom-poisoning? Finally, she blurted out the truth and ran to the phone to call their family doctor. He was out on a call, but his assistant rushed over with stomach pumps. Pandemonium, but the guests were saved.

After they departed, the woman's own doctor finally appeared. "I have to apologize," he said. "I'm afraid I killed your dog. I was on an emergency call and had no time to explain, so I just put him on your porch."

It's quite a story. The only trouble is it never happened. But it refuses to die.

Another story that goes on and on is the one about the couple who received two free tickets to the theater anonymously through the mail. On the evening they planned to use the tickets the husband had to work late so they had to give up their plan to go to the theater. The wife was home alone, doing some ironing, when to her consternation she saw a hand reaching through the mail slot on the door to open it.

Horrified, she realized they had been sent the tickets to get them out of their apartment so it could be burglarized in their absence. Grabbing a hot poker she struck at the hand reaching in to open the door. Then she dashed to the phone to call her friend down the hall and ask for help.

"I can't come," her friend said in a distraught voice. "My husband just came in with his hand horribly burned."

Where do such stories come from? Who makes them up in the first place? No one seems to know. Yet every once in a while someone tells one on our show—as having happened to them or someone they know.

George Burns confessed to me that he has been guilty of making up stories—out of whole cloth and just for fun—and starting them on their mysterious rounds.

"Once I made up a joke about George Jessel telling Joe Frisco how to spell cat," Burns told me. "Someone told Jessel the story and he indignantly denied it. However, the joke started going around and getting a laugh whenever anyone told it. So four months later I ran into Jessel and he greeted me with—'Did you hear the story about me teaching Frisco to spell cat? This'll kill you.' "

On another occasion Burns was driving to Palm Springs with Lou Holtz. Holtz was getting a divorce from his wife and was very depressed. To cheer him up, and avoid a doleful account of marital woes, Burns started telling a long, rambling funny story. It concerned a fictional girl whom Burns supposedly knew, and George told it so elaborately, and with such a wealth of detail, that it lasted all the way to Palm Springs.

When they finally arrived at the desert spa, Burns was exhausted but Holtz was captivated by the story. As they walked into the Racquet Club, Holtz immediately insisted Burns repeat the story, declaring it was the funniest he had ever heard.

Burns demurred, saying it was too long, but Holtz kept insisting. Finally Burns admitted the story was a complete fabrication, and that he had made it up as they drove along just to cheer up Holtz.

"He didn't speak to me for two years," George recalled. "He said he could understand someone making up a story in front of a group of people to get a laugh, but he couldn't understand fibbing to an audience of one."

Tracking down a story or joke is no simple matter. John G. Fuller, who writes a lively column for the *Saturday Review*, once set out to track down a new joke he'd just heard. He got a new notebook, sat down by a telephone, and began his great joke chase in midsummer. Exactly ten weeks and one hundred and six phone calls later, Fuller said he was no nearer the source of the joke, but a lot else had happened. (1) I had told it on the air. (2) It had been printed by someone else in the *Saturday Review*. (3) Several people, by actual count, told it to him in one day. (4) An informant told him he had traced it to the Ziegfeld Follies of 1919. (5) Another informant reported he had traced it to Homer.

With that, Fuller gave up the pursuit.

The *Reader's Digest,* one of my sponsors, also gets a steady stream of stories from the public—all supposedly true. In fact, it seems that most people, when they spot something funny, send it either to the *Digest* or our show, and sometimes both of us get the same story from dozens of people.

The *Digest* reports that a service station near Yellowstone National Park has a drinking fountain named "Old Faceful." Directly under it is a small sign reading, "Don't send this gag to the *Reader's Digest.* It's driving them crazy."

Although people always swear the stories they send in are true, the *Digest,* like myself, has learned to check them carefully. One such concerned a man looking for a used car who saw an ad in a Long Island newspaper offering a nearly new Cadillac for fifty dollars.

At first he dismissed it as a joke, but when the ad continued to appear, he went to look at the car. The address turned out to be a beautiful estate. The owner, an attractive woman, showed him the car and let him drive it. It was too good to be true. After eagerly closing the deal, the man could no longer contain his curiosity.

"Would you mind telling me why you're willing to sell such a beautiful car for fifty dollars?" he asked. "You could easily get several thousand dollars for it."

"Not at all," the woman answered. "In my husband's will were instructions to sell his Cadillac and give the proceeds to his secretary, who had been so kind to him."

The *Digest,* in printing the story, explained that it had suddenly started coming in from all over the country. So far as the *Digest* editors could find out, it had originated in California where the car was a Chevrolet. By the time the story reached New York—where it later appeared in Winchell's column—the locale had shifted to Long Island and the car had become a Cadillac.

The *Digest* did an interesting bit of detective work on another story that had been told to me as true and which I'd used on the show. The story, which had been picked up from the *Providence Bulletin* and sent out nationally by the Associated Press, went like this:

A motorist from Cranston, R.I., sheepishly swears this story is true—but even if it isn't it has to be told. He was driving on the Merritt Parkway when his battery died. He flagged down a woman driver, and she agreed to give him a push to start his car. Because his car had an automatic transmission, he explained to her that she would have to get up to thirty or thirty-five miles an hour to get him started.

The lady nodded wisely. The stalled driver climbed into his car and waited for her to line up behind him. He waited and waited. Then he turned around to see where she was. She was there all right—bearing down on him at thirty-five miles an hour.

Damage to his car: three hundred dollars.

Later the *Bulletin* checked with state police and admitted the story was not true. It had appeared as a joke in a Boston paper, and was phoned in by a prankster to the Providence paper as straight news.

Before the A.P. story appeared, the *Digest* said, it had already received more than one hundred accounts of the incident. They came in from a dozen states and even the Panama Canal Zone, where the car was supposedly on the Trans-Isthmanian Highway. In each case, according to the *Digest,* the writer insisted that the driver was his mother, a neighbor, a close friend or a co-worker.

After the A.P. carried the story, hundreds of clippings poured in. The *Digest* still gets the story occasionally, and so do I. The writers always say they know the people involved.

I once got myself tangled up in this same kind of shell game with the *Digest*. One night I told on the show a true story that happened to me in World War II. While training at Indiantown Gap, Pennsylvania, we were sent out on war games in the rolling Pennsylvania countryside. I was in one of two platoons sent out to hide in the woods, and two others were sent out after nightfall to try to find and "capture" us.

Instead of hiding in the woods with the rest of our platoon, two buddies and I hid behind a signboard and then sneaked down the highway to a diner, where we had hamburgers and chili.

At dawn we crept back into camp with the tired G.I.'s who had mock-battled all night, and I was commended by our captain for eluding capture.

Some viewer heard me tell the story on the air and sent it to the *Digest* which ran it. All he did was change the locale and say that the incident happened to him.

Where do these stories come from, and how do they get started in the first place? It's hard to say. As far back as World War II, when I was entertaining in the jungles, I used to be amazed at the speed with which a joke could travel, even in the midst of a war. I've made up a joke and told it in a jungle on Guadalcanal, only to have it come back to me a couple of days later in a jungle on Bougainville. The G.I. who told it usually claimed it happened to him.

It's interesting to watch the evolution, or sometimes distortion is a better word, of a joke as it travels around, particularly if translation is involved. A classic example is the saying, "The spirit is willing, but the flesh is weak," which was fed into an electric computer during experiments in translation. The computer immediately translated it into Russian, but when a translator put it back into English it came out, "The liquor is still good, but the meat has gone bad."

We have had fun with that kind of experiment on our show. With the assistance of a group of skilled linguists from the Berlitz School, we pass a joke through several languages in rapid succession, and the results are almost always startling. One night, for instance, the joke was this:

"Two birds built a nest with a hole in the bottom. Another bird came along and asked them why. They said they built the nest that way because they were crazy about marriage but didn't want children."

I told the joke to Geneviève in English. She repeated it in French to a Berlitz lady, who then translated it into German for a lady who told it in Spanish to José Melis. Then he told it back to me in English. This is how it came out:

"Two birds built a nest with a hole in the bottom. A bird came along and asked why. They said they built the nest that way because they weren't married."

The moral of these wandering stories seems to be this— the next time someone tells you a story about his uncle's Cadillac in Memphis, be careful. It probably wasn't his uncle, but a second cousin. And it probably was Sheboygan, not Memphis, and most likely it never happened anyway.

Whatever you do, don't send the story to me. By that time someone else will probably have sent it to me and I will have innocently told it on the air. But I promise I won't claim it happened to me.

17

Adventures with the Twelve-year-old Mind

THERE IS a legend that television programs are aimed at a twelve-year-old mentality. I don't know about television, but *I've* spent a lot of time lately aiming at the twelve-year-old mind, since our daughter Randy has now reached that age, and believe me it's a challenge.

Sometimes I think I'll never understand children, and the only solution is for them to grow up so they can understand me. My efforts to follow the mental processes of anyone short of puberty have been maddening, and have led me to agree with Sam Levenson that insanity is hereditary and that we catch it from our children.

When I was growing up, kids had to be nice to their parents. Now parents have to be nice to their kids. I seemed to have missed out coming and going. When I was young we used to think it was a big treat to go down to the A&P and watch them unload the trucks. Or we pulled down the back trolley rope and put the lights out, until they put fishhooks on it and spoiled our fun. Now kids seem to have everything. A lot of them have their own private phones and a couple I know actually learned to count by dialing.

When I was a youngster growing up in Jackson, Michigan, it was a big bang if we got to go to Ypsilanti. Now it's nothing to meet a ten-year-old who has been to Rome or Hawaii, and is very *blasé* about the whole thing.

On one vacation Miriam and I took Randy to Berlin, Vienna, Venice, and the French Riviera, Morocco, Gibraltar and Madrid. She saw a bullfight in Madrid, drifted in a gondola through the canals of Venice, saw bikini-clad beauties on the Riviera, visited the magnificent Schonbrun Palace in Vienna and played with the rock apes at Gibraltar.

When we got home, exhausted, I said to Randy, "We've had three wonderful weeks and you've been to places you probably never dreamed you'd see. What have you learned from it all?"

"I found out that if you want a cuckoo clock," she said, "Munich is the best place to get it."

Practically no one seems quite capable of coping with his children, and it makes me feel a little better to see that this extends to the White House, where Caroline Kennedy frequently steals the limelight from the President of the United States. There's an old show business axiom that a child will always steal a scene from an adult, and the President learned this the time little Caroline teetered out, in her mother's high-heeled shoes, while he was conducting a press conference.

Later, press secretary Pierre Salinger had to publicly muzzle the lively little three-year-old after she told reporters, who asked her what her father was doing, that he was "upstairs with his shoes off, not doing anything."

It isn't just the President, however, who has found himself embarrassed by the diabolical quality of childish frankness. I had it happen once when a friend telephoned just as Miriam and I were sitting down to a before-dinner cocktail. The friend asked Randy, who answered the phone, if her father was busy.

"Oh, no," she said cheerfully. "He's drinking."

Understanding children seems to be formidable at best, and the task is further complicated if the parents are in the public eye. Most of the show business people I know try to shield their children from the limelight, but it isn't easy as I discovered the time I heard one little tyke tell Randy, "My father has a higher Nielsen rating than your father."

Children can scarcely help but get a rather distorted outlook on the world if they can see their father or mother on TV, and some even get the idea you can push a button and see anyone's parents on their TV set if they just know the right channel.

Randy rarely sees my show, since it comes on too late, and I'm just as happy because I'm afraid I might suffer from over-exposure if she had to look at me live *and* on television too.

However, some show business parents I know like to have their children watch them perform. Walter Slezak, my West-chester neighbor, was asked if he let his children stay up to watch TV when one of his old movies appears on *The Late Show*.

"Let them?" he exclaimed. "I *make* them!"

Although Randy doesn't see my show, and prefers *The Un-touchables* anyway, she does take a keen interest in the for-tunes of people who appear on the show, particularly some of the performers we more or less discovered. She always sum-mons me excitedly when someone like Jonathan Winters or Betty White or Betty Johnson appears on another program.

One night during the Presidential campaign, I was in the tub when Randy thumped on the door and yelled, "Come quick, Poppa. One of your discoveries is on television!"

I dried hurriedly, pulled on a robe and rushed to the TV set. There, commentating on the political scene in his crisp, inimitable style, sat H. V. Kaltenborn, the eighty-year-old dean of broadcasting commentators!

There's no doubt, I suppose, that the children of show busi-ness people are even more spoiled than other children, but if there's anything more spoiled than an actor's child it's a child actor. I've encountered some of these deadly little tykes in my day and they seem to combine the worst characteristics of actors and human beings. About the only way to handle them is to send them to bed without their applause.

However, I'm sure that today's children are not entirely to blame for being spoiled, and that parents are also responsible for overindulging them.

Playwright Moss Hart believes in raising children the old-fashioned way, but even he has confessed he has problems with his son, Christopher, eleven. One of them concerns the bathtub and requests to get out of same.

"When are you going to get organized?" Hart demanded one day.

"When I'm about forty-two," the boy replied.

"Well," said Moss, "who's going to support you until then?"

"You are."

"Do you realize," Hart asked sarcastically, "that when you're forty-two I'll be eighty-three?"

"That's okay," Christopher answered. "George Bernard Shaw was still writing when he was ninety!"

Westchester County, where we live, abounds in spoiled children whose idea of a big time is starting fires in mail boxes, handing heated quarters to the Turnpike toll collectors or tossing trash in people's swimming pools. Lately, though, the parents have begun to strike back.

A committee recently approached H. Allen Smith, another Westchester resident, asking that he write something advocating the placing of fences around private swimming pools to protect children. Unfortunately, they called on him just after a group of playful little tads had dumped trash in *his* pool.

Smith turned the committee down flat. "We don't have enough booby traps for kids," he growled. "We should have a few elephant traps around here too."

Smith tells me that kids have a new game—railroad chicken. A group gets on the track when a train is approaching and sees who can stand there the longest before jumping out of the way. "I think," he said, "the railroad has a chance to do a great public service there."

Actually many children today are unspoiled, even children of show people, and some of them turn out quite well despite their parents. Our Randy has been very little trouble, and has always been a good student, and we have never had to use any discipline stronger than threatening to make her watch educational TV. For some reason or other, this seems to have caused a small void in her life.

She came home late from school one day and when Miriam asked why, she said rather proudly, "I was disciplined." The discipline, she declared, consisted of having to stay after class and saddle soap eighteen baseball mitts.

"Eighteen baseball mitts!" Miriam echoed. "What in the world did you do?"

Randy confessed that she had been guilty of the age-old transgression, she had talked in class. Miriam clucked with parental concern and asked what she had been talking about.

"Senator Goldwater," said Randy.

Randy is extremely well informed and frequently makes me look ridiculous by revealing that I don't know the answer to simple questions like the date of the Second Continental Congress or who was Vice President Millard Fillmore. This has happened so often that at one point I began to worry about losing face, and even took to brooding over what I could do to brighten up my father image.

One night, while unable to sleep after watching my show, I was struck by inspiration. The next morning I got up stealthily and carried out my idea . . . and I was an immediate hero! Randy thought I was wonderful and the neighborhood kids looked on me as if I were a combination of Dr. Albert Schweitzer and Frankie Avalon.

Actually what I'd done was very simple. I just bought some explosive caps and Scotch-taped them to Randy's croquet mallets!

Children appreciate simple, thoughtful gestures like that, but most parents spoil their children with lavish gifts like cars. The automobile has become a status symbol for teen-agers and they go to ridiculous lengths to impress each other. I know one little girl who drives around Bronxville in the hottest summer weather with the windows of her sedan closed so the other kids will think she has air-conditioning.

One of the crew on our show told me a story about his son.

He wanted to impress his girl friend who was a student at an upstate New York college, so he rented a car and rode all the way up to see her. When he got home he was horrified to discover he had driven two hundred miles, which was twice as much mileage as he could pay for.

However, he solved the matter rather neatly, I thought. He jacked the car up on blocks, put it in reverse, and let it run until it had erased one hundred miles from the speedometer.

That's the kind of thinking that made America great.

One indulgent show business parent is Nunnally Johnson, the writer and movie producer. Johnson, who has been married three times, has an assortment of children and grandchildren. Some of his children are married and have families of their own, some are not yet married and others are quite small.

"I am the only man in America," Johnson muttered, "who has been reading *Little Black Sambo* for the past thirty-five years."

A show business father who never coddled his children is Charley Weaver. Charley has a grown son named Mike whom he refers to affectionately as "The Bad Seed." Charley says that all the time Mike was growing up he didn't so much as buy him an ice cream cone.

"For years," Charley says, "I told him the Good Humor truck was a fish wagon. I figure I must have saved maybe a thousand dollars that way."

Children are usually not so easily hoodwinked as Charley's "Bad Seed," however, and most of them begin demanding things at an early age. Bob Shanks, who pursues talent for our show, has a cute little five-year-old named Jennifer who recently asked her mother for a mirror.

"I'm getting tired," she said, bitterly, "of making-up in the doorknob."

Most show business people try to join in their children's school and church activities, but this often presents problems.

Let's face it, the P.T.A. meeting isn't quite the same with Gregory Peck reading the minutes of the last meeting, and God never meant for Zsa Zsa Gabor to be a Den Mother. No matter how well intentioned show people may be, I get the feeling that their neighbors tend to look askance if they show up at the church Strawberry Festival.

Gordon and Sheila MacRae have four children and joined the P.T.A. in California, where they live, in an effort to show they were just like all the other parents. One of their sons was so pleased by this that he brought a group of his little friends' parents home to surprise them. When the unannounced delegation arrived, Sheila was out in the back yard swinging upside down from a long cable. She was learning to fly as part of their new nightclub act!

These unannounced arrivals can be unsettling. Randy, who is a gregarious little girl, has a tendency to turn up herself with unexpected company. Once I was shaving in the bathroom when a cute little six-year-old girl wandered in.

Startled to suddenly find a strange child gazing at me, I exclaimed, "Where did *you* come from?"

The child looked puzzled for a moment and then answered proudly, "From America."

I try to take an interest in Randy's activities at school, and attend whatever little functions she is involved in, but there is a certain you-can't-win feeling about it all.

Once I was going to hear Randy play the violin in a class recital. The day of the event I was cleaning our swimming pool and got chlorine in my eyes. Miriam treated them but they were so inflamed that I put on dark glasses to go to the school auditorium.

As we came in, I heard one woman whisper, "Get those dark glasses on Randy Paar's father. Where does the big ham think he is—in Hollywood?"

Annoyed, I pulled off the glasses and sat with my eyes blurred and stinging as Randy came out and played.

"Look at the emotional slob," another lady hissed. "Crying just because his daughter can play the violin!"

One nice thing about schools, though, is that they take over explaining things. After confessing to Randy that there wasn't any Santa Claus, which seemed to cover nearly all questions for some time, I gave up. Randy's school is quite advanced. The children learn about life simply and naturally, by raising little pets as a class assignment. I didn't take too kindly to the idea of her raising a pet at home, but Randy used psychology to get her way.

She came in one day and announced that each child had to raise an animal, and she'd put in for a skunk. Naturally I recoiled at this suggestion. After lengthy negotiation I finally grudgingly agreed to a rabbit.

The rabbit turned out fine, but all did not go as well with some of the other animals. Randy came home one day with a breathless account of one biological experiment that backfired. The teacher had brought in two hamsters, she said excitedly, one male and one female. They were to mate and have offspring, Randy said, but the female ate the male.

"Really," I sympathized. "That's too bad. What did the teacher say about that?"

"He just said, 'Now you know about sex.' "

About the time Randy was raising her rabbit, the aforementioned Jennifer Shanks, who was tired of making-up in doorknobs, was given two turtles by her parents. A few days later she announced she had named one of the turtles "Tonsil."

"Why Tonsil?" her mother asked.

"Because I call the other one Gretel," Jennifer explained.

A little friend of Randy named Toby Campion had a similarly confusing encounter with the nuances in the sounds of words.

Toby's mother is a writer, who wrote *The Long Gray Line* and other books, and some of her literary bent seems to have been inherited by her son, who puts out a little mimeographed neighborhood paper.

The Campions have a neighbor, an eighty-year-old gentleman, who had been in the hospital. Like a true reporter, Toby called the elderly neighbor and interviewed him on his operation.

Mrs. Campion heard her son's end of the phone conversation, which went like this: "Hello, Mr. Jones. This is Toby. I hear you've been in the hospital. Oh, an operation. That's too bad. What was it for? Oh, I see. Well, I'm glad you're feeling better."

Later in the day, Mrs. Campion proofread Toby's first edition as it rolled off the mimeograph machine. Prominent on the first page was a story about Mr. Jones who had been operated on for his *phosphate*.

"Toby sold every issue," Mrs. Campion said. "Mr. Jones bought all the extra copies."

Joey Bishop told me of a somewhat similar story of his son Larry, fourteen, being baffled by the sound of a word, although in this instance the word was swimming in a Southern accent as thick as Creole gumbo.

On our show we have a Bromo Seltzer commercial in which golfer Sam Snead, a West Virginian, speaks of the hazards of the banquet circuit. He then adds, "Ah nevah eat on the day of a tournament."

After the program, Joey's son asked if the golf star was Jewish. "I don't think so," Joey said. "Why?"

"Well," answered his son, "he says in the commercial that he never eats on the Day of Atonement."

18

Don't Call Me, I'll Call You

I'VE BEEN toying with a new invention lately.

It's a telephone that blows up when anyone calls up in the middle of the night and burbles, "I'll bet you can't guess who this is?" I may also fix it so it blows up at the other end on callers who get you out of a hot tub and then get mad because it's the wrong number. Clearly the telephone is getting out of hand.

I'm all for modern conveniences, like electrical can openers, bottled martinis and drip-dry wedding gowns, but the telephone has gotten to be a sheer menace. It isn't the calls you *make* that cause the trouble, but the calls you *get*. My attitude toward the whole problem is summed up in the old showcasting admonition—don't call me; I'll call you.

My resentment toward the telephone started with the singing telegram, and my irritation keeps growing all the time.

Once I got a call from a woman who asked, "How can I find happiness?"

Another time I got a call from a lady who said she was so lonesome she had been taking a bath three times a day hoping the phone would ring.

The nocturnal call is, of course, only one of the many forms of torture which have sprung up since the black day that Alexander Graham Bell's innocent-looking invention made the rack and the thumb-screw obsolete.

Children, like drunks, bring a special dimension to the telephone call. Our daughter Randy being twelve means we can still look forward to the marathon-length calls favored by teen-agers and carried on in pretzel-like positions usually achieved only by advanced practitioners of Yoga.

Walter Slezak, the actor, has a large family of growing children and is a hardened veteran of the telephone talkathon. Recently one of his teen-aged daughters answered the phone and hung up after talking only twenty minutes instead of her usual hour and a half.

"Good for you," he beamed, as she hung up. "That shows what you can do if you try."

"But, Daddy," she said. "It was a wrong number."

One morning, when I was cleaning our swimming pool, I heard the phone ringing. Since no one else was home, I bolted in to answer it, narrowly escaping rupturing myself in my haste to crawl out of the pool.

The caller turned out to be Kathy Reimers, a young friend of Randy's. "I just called up to say happy trip," she announced.

"That's nice, Kathy," I replied, puzzled. "But we're not taking a trip."

"I know," she said, "but I am."

The trials of children's phone calls, however, are minor compared with the frustrations of some business calls. The kind that turn me livid are those where you scramble to the phone to hear a secretary say, sweetly, "Oh, Mr. Paar, I'm terribly sorry. Mr. Bedue is calling you but he just picked up the other phone. I know he'll be with you in just a minute."

You are then supposed to wait patiently while Mr. Bedue, whom you can hear quite plainly, finishes a leisurely discussion with some friend over whether he should get six or six-and-a-half points on the Rose Bowl game. After he settles grudgingly for six points, he finally comes on. By that time, however, I'm back out in the yard pruning the rose bushes.

Many people react to a phone call as if it were a summons to conduct a one-man telethon, with nothing going to charity. Anyone who has ever listened to his wife chat with a neighbor over what they're going to wear to the P.T.A. tea knows what I mean. It took Lincoln less than five minutes to deliver The Gettysburg Address, but it takes two women twenty-five minutes to decide whether one of them should wear her blue silk brocade or two-piece beige wool crepe.

I've become so allergic to this kind of long phone conversation that I've unconsciously developed a galloping telephone manner like a prize-fight announcer. This frenetic delivery saves on nerves and phone bills but sometimes baffles my foreign friends, like Geneviève and José Melis, who have enough trouble understanding English spoken at a leisurely clip.

Once, just before we were going to take the show to Hawaii, I called José, who is my Bronxville neighbor as well as musical director of our show. I was so preoccupied with all the things we had to do that I'm afraid my conversational pace must have been even more revved-up than usual.

"I just heard a great song on the radio," I blurted out as I heard José pick up the phone. "*A Room with a View*. It's perfect for the piano. How about doing it? Incidentally, can you leave three days early for Honolulu so you can rehearse with that Hawaiian band? Oh, and how about turning in two songs instead of one for the days you'll be away, just in case we need them? I'll be by in an hour. I have to go in to rehearsal early today, so if you want to ride with me be ready."

I paused for breath after this torrent of words to see if José had got it all.

Then his voice, tentative and Spanish-flavored, spoke one word. "Alloo?"

In its headlong rush toward progress, the A.T.&T. may soon make life completely unbearable.

I remember, from the Don Ameche movie of fragrant memory, how Alexander Graham Bell invented the telephone. I still vividly recall sitting in the local theater in Jackson, Michigan, watching bug-eyed as Ameche, playing the inventor, spoke the first words ever uttered on the phone.

"Mr. Watson, come here. I want you."

Watson, his assistant, in the next room, popped right in. I've forgotten what Watson said, which is probably just as well, as I'm pretty sure it wasn't anything scintillating.

He probably said, "What do you want me for?" in which case Bell was probably stuck for an answer since he really didn't want him at all. He just wanted to say something on the first telephone, and he wasn't a very inspired ad-libber.

In any case, that was the first telephone conversation, and the quality of the talk hasn't improved much since. You can now get your phone in colors like fuchsia or burnt umber, but you'll find that the conversation that comes out is still as stupefying as ever, whether you take the call in your car or your bathroom.

A man in Indianapolis has invented a "Dial-a-Smile" service, where you dial a certain number and the operator tells you a joke, quickly followed by a commercial. (I knew the commercial people would think of telephones sooner or later.) There is also a new kind of phone on the way which will automatically dial eight hundred and fifty friends, if you happen to have that many.

Phone-answering services will take your calls for you, and there's even a gadget which repeats a recorded message for your friends, if you're out, and records a return message to you.

Hal Kaplow, the author, has one of these and likes to leave whimsical messages. "Hello," the device says, when you ring his number. "This is the recorded voice of Hal Kaplow. The real Hal Kaplow is out gathering material for a quilt."

The voice then gives instructions for callers wishing to leave a message on the recording device, which goes on, after a beep signal, for exactly twenty-six seconds. "Begin to speak when you hear the red light," the voice says. "Remember, I am not responsible for any uncalled-for remarks after thirty days."

A Hollywood producer named Robert P. Newman utilizes the recording device in reverse to bug people he doesn't like.

Newman has a short taped announcement which he uses on his enemies—usually in the middle of the night. The phone rings and the victim sleepily answers it; he hears:

"This call was not intended for you. You may have the wrong party in mind, or perhaps you have answered incorrectly. Please—do not pick up the telephone unless you *know* the call is for you."

Quite a few show business people, I've found, share my antipathy for the telephone. Red Skelton loathes telephones and Oscar Levant once telephoned me all the way from Hollywood just to tell me he never uses the phone. Others in the movie colony virtually live on the phone and call each other constantly.

George Burns has a habit of calling his old friend Jack Benny and then, as a joke, hanging up in the middle of their conversation. This, as might be expected, gets on Benny's nerves.

I first learned about this from George one night when he was a guest on the show. The next night I repeated the story to the audience, then on impulse said, "Why don't I call George Burns right now?"

I picked up the phone on my desk, placed the call and, to my surprise, got him.

"George, this is Jack Paar calling from the studio," I said. "I thought you were great last night, but the New York critics don't seem to agree."

"What do you mean?" George asked anxiously.

"Well, I don't agree with them," I said, "but one of them said that never in thirty-five years was George Burns so . . ."

Then I hung up.

The telephone is getting so highly mechanized these days that it's a pleasant novelty to pick up a phone and get a live operator, especially a friendly one. Perhaps operators can't keep up with the steady march of the phone company engineers any better than the rest of us, and that may be what's making so many of them so irritable lately. Anyway, I've found that the more confusing telephones get, the less helpful operators become.

Joey Bishop told me he once dropped a dime in a phone, completed his call and then got his dime back. The operator rang back instantly and said, "Would you please redeposit your dime?"

"No," Joey said sweetly, "but if you will give me your name and address I'll mail it to you."

Hotel operators seem to be a particularly jaundiced breed, and you have to be on your toes at all times in dealing with them. Marc Connelly, the playwright, tells of an experience he had with a hostile operator when one of his plays was breaking-in out of town. He had worked far into the night making revisions and wanted to leave a late call for the morning. He called the hotel operator and told her he would like to leave a call for twelve noon.

"I'm sorry, sir," the operator said. "We can't make twelve o'clock calls."

"All right," sighed Connelly, "then give me two six o'clock calls."

I've had my own share of conflicts with hotel operators, and one such was occasioned by my penchant for having my home number unlisted. The only telephonic boon, in my opinion, is the unlisted number, and I not only have one but change it oftener than I do my neckties. As a further security measure, to elude lonely ladies, belligerent drunks and other phone pests, I have taken to using an alias when staying at hotels.

Once, while staying at the Beverly Hilton Hotel, I used the name Primrose McGoo, which I had spotted in an H. Allen Smith book I was reading at the time. I walked into my hotel room one afternoon and the light on the phone was flashing, *another* new gadget indicating that someone called while you were out.

I called the operator. "This is Jack Paar. My light was blinking."

There was a long pause. Then the operator said, hesitantly, "This is rather embarrassing, Mr. Paar. Are you staying with Miss McGoo?"

Miriam had flown home to Bronxville to be with Randy for Thanksgiving, so I decided to call and wish them a happy holiday. However, I had just changed my unlisted number and couldn't remember it. I got the Bronxville operator and said, "Honey, this is Jack Paar. I know this sounds crazy but I can't remember my phone number. Would you ring my house for me?"

"Yeah," the operator said, cynically, "that's what they all say."

"I kid you not," I said. "Really, this is Jack Paar. Don't you ever watch the show? Don't you recognize my voice? Listen, I'll hum our theme."

When she hung up midway in the first chorus of *Everything's Comin' Up Roses* I could see it was a losing battle. I got the hotel operator back and asked her to ring my assistant, Mitzi Matravers, figuring she might have my new number.

"I'm sorry," the hotel operator reported presently, "but Miss Matravers has a 'Don't Disturb' on her phone."

"But this is Jack Paar," I protested, getting madder by the minute. "I'm her boss. I've got to talk to her. It's important."

"I'm sorry," persisted the operator. "We have no Jack Paar registered."

"But I *am* Jack Paar," I insisted. "I'm staying right here in room 1120."

"I'm sorry," the operator said sweetly. "Miss Primrose McGoo is registered in room 1120."

19

The Second-oldest Profession

ONE of the occupational hazards of my calling, I discovered long ago, is the press agent. A press agent, to anyone who doesn't know—and they come in pretty confusing guises—is someone who promises to make you famous by getting your name in the paper.

I have always tried to shun the professional ministrations of this gentry, since I seem to have the unfortunate knack of getting my name in the papers when I *don't* want to, but they are multiplying by leaps and bounds and it is hard to escape them entirely. In fact, although I always try to elude their clutches, I have a number of good friends in their ranks and look upon them with the same mixture of awe and dismay with which I regard Willie Sutton, the eminent bank bandit.

Although press agentry is rife in the entertainment world, and some performers surround themselves with virtual platoons of flacks, as *Variety* calls them, press agents now seem to flourish everywhere. They are employed by deposed monarchs, Bulgarian wrestlers, the pretzel industry, society ladies, big business, Chinese restaurants and cemeteries.

The President of the United States employs a press aide in his dealings with the newspapers. Even on the Presidential level dealing with the press seems fraught with some of the same perils and frustrations that beset those who clash the cymbals for cowboy actors or strip-tease artists.

Pierre Salinger, a reformed piano prodigy, told me how he encountered the often amusing confusion of a press secretary's lot even before President Kennedy took office.

On New Year's Eve, 1960, the President-elect was at his father's home in Palm Beach, Florida, while Salinger and the press group covering Mr. Kennedy were at the nearby Palm Beach Towers Hotel. Late in the evening Mr. Kennedy retired and Pierre told the newsmen that there would be no further news that night. Accordingly the press group headed for the hotel bar to welcome the New Year.

However, they had reckoned without Premier Khrushchev of Russia. Shortly before midnight the hotel operator received a telephone call from Washington. A gruff voice in a Gregory Ratoff accent announced that the Russian Embassy had a message for someone to give the President.

The operator put the call through to Salinger's room where there was no one but the press secretary's son, Mark, age twelve. The youngster was flustered by the Russian voice and the name of Khrushchev and ran down the hall to get his pal, ten-year-old Tim Smith, son of veteran White House correspondent Merriman Smith.

Young Smith scooted down to the bar and got his father who took the call. A Russian delivered a New Year's greeting with due solemnity. Then he asked, "May I have your name and rank, please?"

"You'll have to settle for Smith," the White House correspondent said and hung up.

The Khrushchev greeting was announced by Moscow the next day and the reporters in Palm Beach asked the President-elect if he had received the message.

"Yes," smiled Mr. Kennedy, "by a rather circuitous route."

Not only the U.S. government but many foreign countries feel the need of public-relations guidance in dealing with the American public. Some, like the British government, have their own Information Services, while others employ independent Public Relations outfits in an effort to gain a favorable press in this country. *The Reporter* magazine, which has made a detailed study of the extent to which foreign nations use

American public relations firms, says that the practice is growing by leaps and bounds and that U.S. publicity experts are currently engaged in a scramble for the business of the new African nations.

There is nothing wrong with a country using publicity to get favorable attention for itself, of course, but some U.S. newspaper people have taken money from foreign nations to write propaganda in their papers under the guise of "news."

For example, according to *The Reporter,* in 1952 Jack Kofoed, a columnist for the *Miami Herald,* was paid $2,300 monthly, including $800 for expenses, to prepare a book on Dominican Republic dictator Rafael Trujillo, and to write magazine and newspaper articles about him.

"Even his enemies can't deny," Kofoed obligingly wrote in his paper, "that Trujillo has, single-handed, lifted his country from the lowest state it could reach to the place it now occupies." The state it occupied, Kofoed neglected to point out, was an iron-handed dictatorship which was bleeding the Dominican Republic economy white while paying American newspapermen to write about the glories of Trujillo.

Similarly, *The Reporter* disclosed that in 1954 the government of Guatemala hired John A. Clements Associates at a fee of $8,000 a month to handle its press relations in this country. The Justice Department registration showed that the campaign was to be handled by Clements and Patrick McMahon. Clements, interestingly enough, was also editor of the *American Mercury* magazine, while McMahon was the magazine's Washington editor. By a strange coincidence, the magazine ran a number of articles on Guatemala at that time.

I have had an opportunity to observe at close quarters the vigor with which American public relations firms pursue the account of a foreign country. When I talked to Fidel Castro, just after he came to power in 1959, the Cuban dictator seemed in less danger from Batista snipers than from being trampled to death by the American publicists who haunted the Havana Hilton Hotel in hopes of getting Cuba's public relations account. Incidentally, it was discovered after Batista's overthrow that the Associated Press man who covered the Presidential Palace was on the dictator's payroll.

Because I had been going to Cuba for several years before Castro seized power, and because I had interviewed Castro and often spoken of my liking for the Cuban people, some officials from the Cuban Tourist Bureau came to me for advice when relations between Cuba and the United States began to disintegrate.

"You have been so kind to Cuba in the past," one of them said to me, "tell us what we should do to attract American tourists. We will do anything you say."

"My advice," I said, "is for Dr. Castro to get a shave and a dark blue suit."

For some reason, that ended the interview and no country has asked for my advice on public relations since.

The Congressional probe into TV quiz shows revealed rampant skulduggery amid the isolation booths and toppled some public idols. It also provided a colorful insight into the far-flung machinations of publicity people. Each time the probers unearthed some new shenanigan, a press agent was lurking somewhere in the background pulling strings. For every TV idol with feet of clay, some publicity man was acting as chiropodist.

One press agent paid $10,000 to get a contestant on one of the big money shows just to mention the name of his department-store client. Another public relations purveyor forked over a hefty weekly sum to get a cardboard safe, with his client's name on it, on a quiz show where it was seen by millions. One publicity man even managed to get on *Twenty-One* as a contestant himself, and wound up as one of the biggest winners of all!

Although publicity counsel is not always an unmixed blessing, I must confess to a morbid interest in the *modus operandi* of the press agent and I have often watched with fascination as they pursued their machinations.

One of the most ingenious is Ursula Halloran, a pretty brunette who specializes in flacking for comedians. When I was doing *Take It or Leave It* on radio, Ursula was assigned by N.B.C. to handle my press contacts and between us we managed to outrage only a few of the most important columnists and critics. Since then Ursula has gone onward and upward and has fancy offices in the Seagram Building on Park Avenue.

When she first launched her own office, however, she had more modest quarters and a staff consisting of a secretary and one other harried press agent. One summer day she announced she had landed a new client and was bringing him to her office for a meeting. Since Ursula was never given to undue modesty in talking with clients, her lone flack pointed out that the client might be startled to note her meager complement of personnel.

"Just bring in some hats and coats and hang them up," she said unabashed. "I'll tell him that everyone is out on a coffee break."

Her hireling dutifully complied and staggered in with a collection of straw hats, seersucker jackets and other summer attire. The plan worked like a charm and clients thereafter were so reassured by the overburdened hat rack that they were oblivious to the empty desks.

Ursula subsequently flew to California for a rather lengthy sojourn. When she walked into her office on her return she took one look at the groaning hat rack and had a fit.

"Haven't you any brains?" she demanded of her startled flack. "Don't you know it's winter? Get rid of those straw hats and seersucker jackets and get some umbrellas and galoshes and overcoats. What will our clients think!"

As that story indicates, Ursula is a quick thinker who could give ad-libbing lessons to some of her comedian clients. Another time, when she was publicizing the *Medic* TV show, she got a call from a TV columnist who asked what a forthcoming episode of the program would deal with.

She didn't know, so she clapped her hand over the phone and whispered to her flack, "What's the next episode of *Medic* about?"

"It's about euthanasia," her associate whispered back.

"It's about euthanasia," she said breezily over the phone. "It's a wonderful show . . . very dramatic."

"What in hell is euthanasia?" asked the TV columnist.

"Oh, you know," Ursula said, confidently. "It's all about the young people in the Orient."

Despite low fees and high blood pressure, most of the press agents I know retain remarkably resilient spirits. Mack Millar is one of this bulldog breed. Once, when Mack was publicizing a Las Vegas nightclub, he got into an argument with the owner. The proprietor slugged Mack, flooring him. Mack got up with dignity and dusted himself off.

"I'll take that," he announced, "as my two weeks' notice."

In view of the peculiar nature of publicity, it is no wonder that even its practitioners have trouble defining it, although one cynical flack terms it "the second-oldest profession."

As someone who has seen a good deal of ballyhoo in all its forms, I have a tendency to shudder at the pomposity of the growing field called public relations, and retain a sort of grudging respect for the hearty souls who manage to cadge newspaper or air space merely through fiendish ingenuity, persistency or sheer gall.

One of this shrinking band of free souls is Jim Moran, an unabashed press agent of the old school.

An example of the Moran technique was his stunt on behalf of a product called "X-M," designed to keep people's eye glasses from fogging up. To publicize his spectacle de-fogger, the bearded flack turned up in Washington, D.C., with a hundred homing pigeons. They were like any other homing pigeons, except that each was equipped with miniature spectacles.

"I am going to free these homing pigeons," Jim announced to the assembled press. "As you can see, they are all wearing spectacles. Half of the spectacles have been treated with 'X-M,' half have not. I am willing to wager that those whose glasses have been treated with this fine product will get home quicker and safer than those whose spectacles have not been so treated."

Sure enough, the fifty birds with "X-M" on their tiny glasses headed home to New York as straight as arrows, while the others fluttered about erratically and took off in all directions. One eventually turned up in Steubenville, Ohio, looking as if it had been trapped on the way in a badminton game.

Skeptics have since charged that the fifty pigeons with the untreated glasses weren't homing pigeons at all, but Moran has never dignified this accusation with an answer. In any case, "X-M" got off to a flying start.

Another of the legendary stunt men is my friend Tom Ferris, an Irish-born flack who has now reformed and is the dignified public relations director for the Mackle Brothers, a trio of builders who own a chunk of Florida larger than Guatemala.

One of the stories told about Ferris concerns Gar Wood, the late speed-boat king. When Tom was in charge of publicizing the city of Miami Beach, he got a wire from a man in New York. It read: "Please wire how old Gar Wood is."

Ferris wired back: "Old Gar Wood is fine. How you?"

Ferris once decided to stage a fake drowning to publicize Harvey Stone, the comic, who was appearing at a local hotel. Stone, an excellent swimmer, objected violently but Ferris eventually persuaded him to go along.

Tom staged his drowning craftily. Waiting until the local press were gathered at a beachfront hotel interviewing a Supreme Court Justice, he gave the signal. Stone swam out beyond the breakers and began to flap his arms wildly and yell for help.

The hotel lifeguard plunged in to rescue the supposedly sinking comedian. Lifeguards from other hotels joined in the rescue and when the seemingly water-logged Stone was dragged ashore hundreds of people had gathered, including a half-dozen photographers from the nearby press conference.

The lifeguard hauled Stone up on the sand, dropped him face-down and began to administer artificial respiration. At this point another comedian, Jackie Miles, who was playing a rival hotel, noticed that the apparent victim was his fellow comic Stone.

Not being in on the fraud, Miles dropped down on the sand beside Stone and said emotionally, "Speak to me, old pal."

By this time all the photographers were popping pictures, but all they were getting were shots of Jackie Miles and Stone's back, half-buried in the sand.

Ferris was stunned by this disastrous turn of events. Kneeling down by the soggy Stone, he whispered, "Miles is grabbing all the pictures. Turn over."

Stone tried to, but the husky lifeguard and Miles were still on top of him enthusiastically squeezing all the wind out of him.

After his stint hymning the glories of Miami Beach, Ferris was hired by the Mackle Brothers and has assumed a dignity and calm that is a far cry from his old days of flacking. At times, however, he still shows a flash of his old irreverence.

Once he was showing me through the beautiful new Mackle Building. In one office he found an executive under his desk adjusting an electric wire. All we could see were the man's feet, toes up, extending from under his desk.

"This is one of our auditors," Ferris airily explained. "He has a little problem with early morning drinking."

Perhaps one reason I get a certain satisfaction out of the chicanery of press agents, and especially the wild publicity stunt, is that I enjoy seeing newspapers taken in. Whenever I find a newspaper holding forth on the shortcomings of television, I think happily of how often they have fallen for some preposterous stunt hatched by Jim Moran or Tom Ferris. And their columnists, like Walter Winchell and Dorothy Kilgallen, would soon run dry were it not for the hordes of anonymous flacks crouched over typewriters in dingy offices making up, out of sheer imagination, the items that will be breathlessly passed along by these famous columnists.

A wonderful example of the gullibility of newspaper columnists involved Jack Tirman, a fast-talking Broadway flack, who once found himself saddled with the task of publicizing the attractions of an obscure Greenwich Village café, which didn't have any.

It was obvious he would have to resort to guile. Accordingly he made up a dance team with the improbable name of Gomez and Weinberg, and began bombarding the columnists with the imaginary activities of his fake terpsichorean team.

Soon items began to find their way into print. One column reported that Gomez and Weinberg had been held over. Another chronicled that they were expecting a blessed event. Still another disclosed they had split up. Almost every paper paid tribute to their dancing and mentioned the night spot where they were supposedly appearing.

Only a columnist of the New York *Post* held out. Emboldened by success, Tirman called the columnist and asked why he wasn't using the items he was sending in on Gomez and Weinberg.

"I've seen their act," snarled the columnist, "and they're lousy."

I must admit that publicity people use blandishments as well as ingenuity in courting the press, flying newspaper reporters around on elaborate junkets and throwing lavish parties in their honor. They also rely on gifts to assure the good will of newspaper columnists. On one occasion a group of flacks was sitting outside Dorothy Kilgallen's office waiting to be summoned when a cockroach crawled across the floor and under the door.

As the roach disappeared, one of the press agents spied it and growled, "Hey you, get back in line."

20

Had Argument, Will Travel

TRAVEL is getting easier all the time; it's the traveler who keeps getting more difficult. You can fly now and pay later, or go any place from Addis Ababa to Zanzibar on your Diner's card. You can even—as I discovered the night of February 12, 1960—get all the way to Hong Kong by telling a questionable joke. The secret words in my case were "water closet."

The next thing I knew the stewardess was saying, "Please fasten your seat belts," and our big jet was sweeping in over the teeming harbor for a landing in the incredible city of Hong Kong. Last time it took a world war to get me to the Pacific, and this time I made it on just a small dispute.

Before I discovered the magic properties of the phrase "water closet" as a launching propellant, I had never traveled extensively. Even in New York, I never go south of Luchow's restaurant. I had taken my wife, Miriam, and our twelve-year-old daughter, Randy, to places like Nassau and Bermuda. We also made several trips to Cuba, including one ill-will tour on which I interviewed Fidel Castro, but I'd never been on an extended trip except when the Army dispatched me to Guadalcanal in World War II, and that was scarcely a vacation.

However, when I walked off our show in a dispute over the W.C. joke, I headed for Hong Kong and Miriam and I turned into world travelers. We discovered how fascinating travel can be, even on the hit-and-run itinerary dictated by a television schedule, and we've been devout tourists ever since.

You don't get to know the natives well, or to plumb the culture, when you travel as fast as we do, but you do meet the most interesting bellhops. Also, I've discovered in the course of our travels that it's possible to strain international relations in even a brief stay in a foreign country.

Paul Keyes, my head writer, who has accompanied me on several of my treks, once summed up our travels by sighing, "I've fought my way out of nine countries with Paar."

It isn't that I deliberately court trouble. It's just that I seem to be disaster prone, and strange languages, foreign currency and exotic drinks don't help any. In any event, I've kept a little diary of our travels. It's a sort of running account of our trips around the world and, believe me, it seemed as though we were running most of the time.

Before taking off for Hong Kong, after my tiff with the N.B.C. censor, about all I knew about China was what I had absorbed from reading the messages in Chinese fortune cookies and some of them are as inscrutable as the mysterious Orient itself. In fact, I once got one that I still worry about.

It said merely, "Disregard previous fortune cookie."

Hong Kong burst upon Miriam and me with a stunning impact. It seemed then, and still does in retrospect, the most unusual and exciting city we had ever seen. From the moment we stepped off the plane, at Kai Tak airport, we found ourselves in an amazing and utterly different new world of startling colors, quaint sounds and pungent smells.

The city itself, officially called Victoria, is on Hong Kong island, which is slightly larger than the island of Manhattan. The whole Colony, however, includes about two hundred and fifty other smaller islands as well as the Kowloon Peninsula and the New Territories on the mainland of China, across the bay from Hong Kong island.

There is no bridge between Hong Kong island and the mainland. You make the trip in ferries which weave their way swiftly among the Chinese junks, tugs and foreign ships that crowd the harbor. Hong Kong's problems are many, from the flood of refugees from Communist China, just a few miles away, to the menace of hit-and-run rickshaws, but the city is gay, bustling, cosmopolitan and beautiful.

Wandering around, we found ourselves almost swallowed up in a riot of noise and color. The blast of pneumatic drills blended with the mournful notes of brass bands playing funeral dirges in the winding streets, and the sing-song shouts of street peddlers mixed with the sputtering of firecrackers heralding anything from the birth of a baby to the opening of a new laundry.

We had a wonderful host and guide in James Robinson, N.B.C.'s Hong Kong correspondent, and his lovely wife, who showed us through the maze of wonders of the pulsating city. With the Robinsons we rode the funicular railway to admire the magnificent view from the towering peak which dominates the city, poked through the thieves market in Cat Street and dodged rickshaws on Gloucester Road in the garish waterfront quarter—the world of Suzie Wong.

Miriam and I were both tremendously interested in the history and culture of the Colony, and we bombarded Jim with a host of questions. Miriam wanted to know the population, the future of the refugee problem, the extent of the opium traffic and the threat of Red China. After impatiently waiting a polite interval, I asked what we really wanted to know— where could we get some real bargains?

Like most tourists, I suppose, the other wonders of Hong Kong seemed not as astonishing to us as the fact that watches are cheaper here than in Switzerland, cameras cost less than in Germany, and you can get a fine custom-tailored man's suit that would cost one hundred and fifty dollars in the United States for thirty-five dollars.

The Robinsons obligingly led us to a cheerful Chinese tailor, where I was able to get a beautifully tailored suit in one day. I was measured after breakfast, had my first fitting before lunch, second fitting after lunch and was all togged out in a fine new suit for dinner that night.

Both Miriam and I are devout shoppers, so we had a field

day in Hong Kong, with its thousands of shops with bargains in silks, furniture, cameras, jade and a hundred other things.

In fact, we saved so much money on all our purchases that in just a few days we were practically broke!

Eating, like shopping, is truly an adventure in Hong Kong, where they have the most bizarre Chinese dishes, in addition to the finest Western cuisine. Before our visit all I knew about Chinese cuisine I learned from being raised on Cantonese cooking—in Canton, Ohio, where I was born.

However, Jim Robinson is a veteran of the Far Eastern gastronomic front and he steered us around with finesse. He even introduced us to chop sticks and we soon discovered that eating with them is a little like knitting a meal. He usually ordered for us, cautioning us never to order bear claws or snake soup in the summertime, or people would think we were tourists.

One dinner ordered by Jim included chunks of Peking duck wrapped in a kind of rubbery pancake, a soup made from the duck's innards and for dessert a candy-coated apple sprinkled with sesame seeds. If we wished, Jim volunteered, we could also sample such local delicacies as sea slugs, chow dog puppies in bean sprouts or monkey brains, but we politely declined. I'm all for East meeting West but, after listening to Jim's description of the menu, I decided that never the twain shall eat.

On another memorable evening the Robinsons took us by sampan to a huge floating restaurant. The restaurant was a blaze of lights from lanterns and glimmering strings of fluorescent tubes, and we had a choice of catching our own dinner or selecting it from an assortment of blue lobsters, brightly hued parrot fish, conch or abalone. As we dined we looked out over the surrounding harbor, with its thousands of sampans.

Jim also wanted us to sample a truly Chinese restaurant and selected one in an out-of-the-way section of Kowloon. It was so quaint and completely Chinese that it was obvious the sight of a white man was a rarity. This was evident as we walked in and the Chinese musicians began to point and whisper.

"They recognize you are an American," Jim said, "and they want to play something appropriate."

As he spoke, the orchestra broke into a sing-song, oriental version of, of all things, "Silent Night."

Hearing "Silent Night" on a February afternoon in Kowloon was a note of incongruity which seemed to typify Hong Kong, a city of vivid contrasts. It is bustling and prosperous, with the streets and shops crowded with well-heeled tourists and busy Chinese, yet it is also filled with poor refugees who escape from nearby Red China at the rate of a thousand a week.

The refugees sleep on the sidewalks or roofs or boats, or build pitiful shacks out of cardboard and tin cans next to fashionable, air-conditioned apartment houses. Yet they manage to survive, somehow, and their happy children are the liveliest and most charming I have seen anywhere in the world.

Red China could easily gobble up Hong Kong, whose tallest building is the seventeen-story Communist Bank of China, yet the British still control the Colony and evidences of their chin-up existence, amid three million Chinese, are seen in the Cricket Club and the office of Thomas Cook and Son, where at noon they post the delightfully English sign—"Closed for tiffin."

From Hong Kong we took a boat overnight to the Portuguese colony of Macao, forty miles across the South China Sea. Macao is widely known as a sinful city, but to us it seemed about as sinful as Nutley, New Jersey, on a rainy Sunday. It, too, was jammed with refugees, but lacked the color and vitality of Hong Kong. The poverty on every hand was terribly saddening.

We visited a Chinese temple where a priest told my fortune by shaking some sticks in a can. "Sir, you are a pine tree," he announced, after looking over his jumble of sticks. "Your worst season is the winter, because you're apt to be chopped down."

Since it was then midwinter, and I was feeling rather chopped down after walking off my show, the Chinese priest was getting too close for comfort.

At least he seemed more prophetic than those fortune cookies I had been relying on for advice.

During our visit in Hong Kong, we stayed at the Miramar Hotel in Kowloon, across the bay from Hong Kong island. The service was excellent, with hordes of white-clad Chinese waiters padding about in black coolie slippers, but Hong Kong was suffering from a water shortage and there was water for bathing during only a couple of hours in the afternoon. As a result, our bathing was carefully scheduled.

One morning, however, I noticed the hot water tap leaking and out of curiosity turned it on. To my astonishment, a stream of hot water gushed out. I tried the cold tap. Not a drop. Cheered by the unexpected dividend of hot water, I hurriedly filled the tub to the brim with steaming water and triumphantly called Miriam.

I stuck a cautious finger into the water and found it still hot enough to boil lobsters. We then made the discovery, no doubt long known to science, that scalding water takes a long time to cool. We stood around on one foot and then on another, but the water remained maddeningly hot. We had to go out early, and were eager for baths.

Finally, the two of us wound up kneeling by the tub and patiently blowing on it, as if it were a bowl of minestrone.

Before leaving we went to look at the vast, grim bulk of the Red Chinese mainland, hanging like a dark cloud over beautiful Hong Kong. We drove twenty miles from Kowloon through the New Territories to a point where a barbed-wire fence and a few soldiers in mustard-colored uniforms mark the border of Red China.

On the drive we wound through a quilt-work of cultivated fields, worked by brown-skinned men and women wading through rice paddies, among blue hills where the bones of the dead are bleached in stone jars.

At the border, officials gave me big binoculars so I could look across the border and see what the Communists were doing.

What I saw was a Communist soldier with big binoculars looking back at me!

21

Altogetherness in Japan

TOKYO has the largest population of any city in the world, but it won't have for long. Not with those taxi drivers. The cab drivers of Tokyo, I quickly discovered, seemed to be ex-*kamikaze* pilots who had neglected to *kamikaze* themselves and were carrying out a last ditch offensive against pedestrians and other drivers.

The last time I had encountered the Japanese, before our trip to Tokyo, was on Guadalcanal in World War II, and they haven't gotten noticeably friendlier since. At least the taxi drivers haven't. They whip through the crowded streets of Tokyo with an utter abandon that outdoes the wildest drivers of New York, the suicidal motorists of Paris and the Freeway freedom fighters of Hollywood.

Actually, the wild driving of Japanese cabbies seems to spring from one of the national virtues—an obsession about being punctual. The Japanese make a fetish of being on time, and taxis seem determined to get to their destination *ahead* of time.

The Japanese preoccupation with being on time also extends to their trains. The Japan National railways are so proud of maintaining schedules that if a train is late, which almost never happens, the railroad passes out certificates to their passengers, stating how late the train was. Workers then present these to their employers, who otherwise would probably never believe them.

Miriam and I took a train from the resort area of Hakone, near Fujiyama, and were surprised to notice that all the other passengers set their watches as the train departed. The train was scheduled to leave at eleven-fifteen A.M., and apparently none of the passengers had any doubt that it was *exactly* eleven-fifteen when we pulled out.

Like all the other passengers, I dutifully set my watch for eleven-fifteen too, although I couldn't quite match their faith in a railroad's infallibility. I've been a commuter on the New York Central too long.

Aside from the trains, which do run forward, practically everything in Japan runs backwards, or at least opposite from the way ours work. For instance, Japanese books begin at the back and read forward. Also, in some of their books, you read from left to right. In other words, if this book were in Japanese you might be reading it upside down and backwards, and it might read even better that way.

Since I confuse rather easily, we were fortunate in having Cecil Brown, N.B.C.'s Far Eastern correspondent, and his charming wife, Martha, as our hosts and guides through the inside-out culture of the Japanese.

It's practically impossible, we found, driving around with the Browns, to locate a house in Tokyo—at least by the address. For one thing, streets have no names. Also, houses are numbered in the order in which they were built. Consequently, you may find house number 1 next to 379, while number 2 is a mile away down a winding alley.

To compound the confusion, many houses have the same address. On one estate, once owned by a Japanese prince, there are now a half-dozen four-story apartment houses and more than one hundred homes, each with the same address!

The Japanese telephone service can be mighty confusing too, we discovered. While staying at the Imperial Hotel in Tokyo, I had occasion to call my office in New York several times. For these calls I used a special network line called a tieline.

Toward the end of our stay Tom Cochran, my associate

producer, telephoned the Imperial to ask what plane we were returning on and was a little startled to be told I had "gone to Thailand." Since my itinerary has been known to become rather erratic on occasion, Tommy shrugged philosophically and began trying to track me down in Bangkok.

After some involved conversations, in a variety of Oriental accents, he discovered I was still in my room at the Imperial contemplating the mysteries of the inscrutable East.

What the operator had said, after her Japanese accent was unscrambled, had been, not that I had "gone to Thailand," but that I was "talking on tieline."

Other aspects of Japanese life are equally perplexing. Japanese men, I discovered, admire petite girls with flat chests and boyish features. This, Cecil Brown explained to me, is probably because Japanese women get their ideals of beauty from the Kabuki theater, where feminine roles are played by men. Marilyn Monroe, Jayne Mansfield and other actresses widely admired in America for their generous physical endowments are pitied in Japan, while Audrey Hepburn, whose curves are roughly comparable to those of Tony Perkins, is muchly admired.

Incidentally, Japanese women shave. They shave their face, forehead, neck, chin and even ears on the theory that it keeps their skin soft—and it seems to work.

American TV shows, particularly westerns and situation comedies with dubbed dialogue, are popular in Japan, but their television does have its own distinctive character. One of their early morning wake-up shows, for example, features three-minute recordings of bird twitterings. As one who has never gotten any overpowering message from bird calls, even on Ted Mack's Amateur Hour, it seems to me that being awakened at six twenty-seven in the morning by shrill chirpings may account for the prevalence of *hari kari* in Japan.

Japanese popular music, unlike their movies, which are not

only more numerous but frequently better than ours, is almost entirely imitative of American music.

Japanese singers, who look like caricatures of Elvis Presley and Fabian, sing by rote lyrics learned from American records. Believe me, you've never heard anything until you hear a Japanese singer wailing: "Rove me or reave me, or ret me be ronery."

Japan makes more movies than Hollywood (542 Japanese versus 151 American in 1960), but our pictures are extremely popular there. However, the titles undergo some quite bizarre changes when they are translated into Japanese. *Anne of Brooklyn* became *Love Should Be Quick* on Japanese marquees, *Enjoy the Night* turned into *Pillow Talk* and *A Hole in the Head* came out *Tears and Waves Are Both Warm!*

Japanese signs generally have an air of endearing wackiness about them. In one Tokyo hotel I saw one which proclaimed:

"Pan American Flight number 2, scheduled to depart today for Honolulu, has been postponed indefinitely. It will leave tomorrow."

I am always interested in exploring the culture of a country, so while in Tokyo I went to an *Onsan*, or public bath for men. Mixed bathing in the nude is also popular in Japan, where they apparently believe not only in togetherness but in altogetherness, but I decided to skip the coeducational splashing. But I discovered that even in an *Onsan* the men bathe assisted by lady attendants who wear costumes that might have been borrowed from the chorus line at the *Copacabana*.

Bathing in my pelt in front of a lady was a little too much for my Presbyterian upbringing, so with an exaggerated loyalty to one of my sponsors, I took the plunge attired in jockey shorts. The cute little almond-eyed attendant seemed rather startled by this outburst of modesty but accepting my eccentric behavior with Oriental fatalism proceeded to scour me with something that must have been "Brand X."

The Japanese, I learned during her ministrations, never use

soap *in* the bathtub. She soaped me vigorously, then rinsed me off before I got into the tub. She also baked me in a steam box, scrubbed me with seaweed and finally gave me a masage and did my nails.

The *pièce de résistance* was getting dressed again. The Japanese take great pride in the most minute detail, and my pretty attendant took six or seven minutes just to tie my shoe laces, achieving an effect as elaborate and ornate as a flower arrangement.

The only trouble was that as soon as I got back to the hotel I had to untie her beautiful knots so I could take off my shoes and get out of my soggy shorts.

Having sopped up an odd assortment of Japanese lore, I could hardly wait to get home so I could try it out on someone. The ideal victims, we decided, would be my old friend Jack Douglas and his new wife, a charming Japanese singer. Reiko, the daughter of a Buddhist priest, doesn't speak much English but learns our songs phonetically and belts them out in a voice once described as sounding like "an aroused Teresa Brewer."

I first became acquainted with Reiko's shortcomings in English when I had her and Jack as guests on the program shortly after their marriage. Jack explained that although his bride spoke little English he had coached her on questions he thought I might ask. This assurance from the maniacal Douglas should have put me on guard, but didn't.

"Well," I asked the beaming bride, "what have you been doing in America?"

"Me been photographing military installations," she announced in utter innocence.

So on our return from Tokyo, we invited the Douglases to our home for a Japanese dinner and a movie in our projection room. The pretty Japanese bride seemed to enjoy the dinner. Afterward, as we headed for the screening, I remembered in sudden panic that the movie I had planned to show was *The Bridge on the River Kwai*—a picture in which Sessue Hayakawa plays a cruel Japanese prison-camp commander, and which ends with William Holden blowing up a trainload of Japanese. However, it was too late then to do anything.

I sat cringing at the harsh reminder to the dainty Japanese bride of the bitter wartime feeling between her country and ours.

At the end of the picture, as we left the projection room, I sidled up to Jack and whispered that I was sorry for my thoughtlessness.

"That's all right," he said, "I told Reiko they were Indians."

22

My War with Hawaii

WE VISITED HAWAII not long after the beautiful group of islands which stretch out over 300 miles in mid-Pacific had become our fiftieth state, and managed, with the best intentions in the world, to strain our newly cemented relationship. In fact, I think I got the most hostile reception of any visitor since Captain James Cook in 1779, who was greeted with such wild enthusiasm by the natives that he succumbed of multiple abrasions and contusions inflicted by the welcoming committee.

We telecast our show from the colorful Hawaiian Village hotel the night of the Presidential election, with the outcome still in doubt. On the program I mentioned having wired Richard Nixon. "Congratulations on your overwhelming victory. In case you lost, please call Jack Kennedy and read this to him."

In referring to the election, I inadvertently said, "Back in the United States . . ."

Well, you'd think from the uproar that I'd impugned the memory of King Kamehameha or misspelled Hawaii's favorite fish—the *humumunukunukuapuaa*. At first, when the audience laughed, I didn't know what they were laughing at. Then someone in the audience yelled that since Hawaii was now part of the United States, I should use the word "mainland" in referring to the forty-eight states.

I got their point, although I couldn't understand why they were so touchy.

I certainly meant no harm. I tried to explain that it was

183

hard to get used to the fact that people in hula skirts and *muu muus* were Americans. "After all," I pointed out, "you were the first state to join the Union in your underwear."

However, like most converts, the new citizens were extremely thin-skinned and matters weren't helped much when I made the same slip a couple of more times during the show.

Despite my protestations that my mistake was inadvertent and probably due to upper plate wobble, the Honolulu papers were up-in-arms the next day. They took umbrage at my innocent remarks and the Honolulu *Advertiser* reported that the audience had booed me.

This simply was not true, as our tape of the show proved, but it indicated that Hawaii had certainly earned statehood in one respect. Their papers, obviously, were just as inaccurate as ours back on—steady now, I must get this right—the *mainland*. (Ah, there, I finally got it! Honolulu papers please note.)

After the papers had aired their wounded feelings and their low opinion of the barbaric mainlanders on our show, Eddie Sherman, a Honolulu columnist and broadcasting personality, invited me to go on Henry Kaiser's TV and radio station and give my side of the story. I said I'd be glad to, and I hoped the newspaper people who had written about the incident would be on hand so we could straighten out the facts and soothe the delicate sensibilities of the Hawaiians.

As I suspected, the newspaper people didn't turn up, so I had to unburden myself on the low state of Hawaiian journalism with no rebuttal. The show was broadcast on radio as we did it and was taped for showing later on TV. People began hearing it on their car radios, and started flocking to the station, so that by the time we finished the broadcast the studio was crowded with people apparently enjoying the controversy.

Henry Kaiser, the famous tycoon, was having dinner for our group that night at his palatial home near Koko Head and we and the other dinner guests listened when it was rebroadcast later that evening.

After the show, Miriam called to thank the station for giving me a chance to air my side of the rumpus. Her call was put through to an announcer who was on the air, so that their conversation was broadcast as they talked.

Before long both the telephone and the tropical drinks were being passed rather freely around the Kaiser living room, and soon Peggy Cass, Charley Weaver and other guests were airing their views of the dispute. Even Henry Kaiser, who sat looking like a bemused Buddha, had his say, although I never did figure out exactly what it was he said.

One member of our party summed up the controversy particularly well, I thought:

"I want to tell you about this dear boy, Jack Paar," he said. "I've known him forty-odd years, and I don't see why anyone should criticize him. I don't think this wonderful man would knowingly offend anyone, particularly our glorious new fiftieth state."

This splendid summary of the situation, I have been assured by eye-witnesses, was uttered by none other than me! You can't prove it by me, for by that time I had imbibed several *mai tais*, a deceptively lethal concoction of rum and pineapple which tastes as innocent as an ice-cream soda but packs the impact of a Hawaiian war club, and my memories of the evening are mercifully hazy.

I do vaguely remember getting a personally conducted tour by Kaiser of his spectacular two-million-dollar home, including the two, carpeted, air-conditioned, sound-proofed kennels for Mrs. Kaiser's thirty poodles, complete with trophy room, maternity ward and beauty salon. I also recall introducing Buddy Hackett to Kaiser.

As they shook hands, the rotund comic asked the former head of the defunct Kaiser-Fraser automobile company, "Do you know where I could get a set of sparkplugs for a 1947 Kaiser two-door?"

I also learned a fine old Hawaiian expression, "Licky poo," which, it seems, means "one more." My memory of the latter part of the evening is rather cloudy, but I do remember that things got somewhat boisterous as the night progressed.

Peggy Cass lost one of her contact lenses in a dish of Passion Fruit sherbet, a couple of guests, in evening clothes, almost drowned trying to emulate Duke Kuhanamoku in the huge, Olympic-size pool, and I tried to organize an expedition to leave at once for Hong Kong.

However, Henry Kaiser apparently felt there was no use in estranging Hong Kong too, and managed to talk me out of my precipitous departure for the Crown Colony.

In spite of our little skirmish with the sensitive inhabitants of our fiftieth state, we had a wonderful time in Hawaii. The climate is delightful, the scenery is lush, and the people are friendly, when not aroused.

Honolulu is changing, though, and the soft winds bearing the scent of *pikake* blossoms are giving way to the blast of riveting hammers as new hotels sprout on every hand. The new buildings, like the scenery, feature the lush and bizarre. In one hotel you take the elevator *down* to your room (It is built down the side of a cliff.) and there is a revolving bar atop the twenty-five-story Ala Moana building, where you can get dizzy without even drinking.

The Hawaiian Village, where we stayed, was built by Henry Kaiser. It embraces a clutch of thatched-roof cottages, five hotels of assorted sizes and shapes and a hospital to house the overflow from the hotels. This latter may be the only place anywhere where a guest can ring room service and get his temperature taken.

The Hawaiian Village also has five swimming pools, six cocktail lounges and more than fifty shops. Kaiser has some sort of fixation about pink and almost everything about the place is pink, including some of the guests who have been out in the sun too long.

Kaiser discovered Hawaii a few years ago, after a colorful career making ships, dams, cars and money, and now seems to control more territory in the Pacific than anyone since General Douglas MacArthur. Even with his large collection of palm-clad real estate, I got the impression that he is still not satisfied. I suspect that as soon as he can train the beachboys, he plans to invade the mainland.

Since our visit, Kaiser sold the Hawaiian Village to Conrad Hilton, and it is now called the Hilton Hawaiian Village, but the seventy-nine-year-old tycoon is not exactly lolling around on the beach at Waikiki. In fact, he gets up each morning at five to inspect the progress of the four-hundred-million-dollar city, called Hawaii Kai, that he is building on the former salt marshes and volcanic slopes near his home on the eastern end of Oahu island. Like all of Kaiser's Hawaiian knickknacks, including his hotels, bulldozers, dredges and catamarans, the homes in Hawaii Kai will be shocking pink.

The *kamainas*, or long-time residents, are not taking kindly to these signs of progress, and we heard a good deal of dark muttering during our stay. Kaiser's pink dream of progress, many of the *kamainas* grumbled, is turning the languid island of Oahu into a strand as gauche as Miami Beach, and Waikiki may soon be as crowded as Coney Island on the Fourth of July.

I noticed myself that even the ocean was getting overcrowded at Waikiki Beach. This situation was dramatized when Duke Kuhanamoku, the famous swimmer who is as much a Hawaiian landmark as Diamond Head or the swivelling behinds of the hula dancers, was wounded by a hit-and-run surfboard rider.

Hawaii is a wonderful place to forget your everyday worries, and I suspect that Charley Weaver, Peggy Cass, Paul Keyes and the rest of our group may have had ideas, after a few *mai tais*, of abandoning themselves to the spell of the tropics. However, a Presbyterian convention was meeting at the hotel while we were there, which put something of a damper on any ideas we may have had about going native.

The church delegates set a stern example for us all, although it was rather strange to be kept awake at night listening to "The Old Rugged Cross," played on conch shells and bongo drums.

Speaking of music, I think I liked everything about Hawaii except the everlasting twanging of electric guitars. One night, after our return, I was explaining to Peter Ustinov the maddening effect of the never-ending electric guitars.

"When," he asked, "did they change from gas to electricity?"

Hawaii has some wonderfully colorful customs. For instance, the word "Aloha" means both "hello" and "good-by," which accounts for some very short phone conversations.

Flowers grow in glorious profusion in the tropical climate, and they serve orchids with everything, like parsley. If you order a drink it arrives with an orchid in it. I ordered eggs for breakfast and even they arrived with an orchid on the plate. When I sent out my laundry, I half-expected it to come back with an orchid adorning my jockey shorts.

Despite the lavish way in which the Hawaiians use orchids, the hibiscus is the official state flower. A charming old custom of Hawaii, we found, is that ladies use the hibiscus to indicate their availability.

When a girl wears a flower over her *left* ear, it was explained to us, that means she is available. When she wears one over her *right* ear, however, it means she is already taken. We heard one sad story of a plain little school teacher from Oklahoma who saved up for years to come to the romantic atmosphere of Honolulu in the hope of finding a nice man. Then, when she got there, she mistakenly put the flower behind the wrong *ear*. Not only did she not find her man, but the hotel clerk charged her for a double room.

Another of the charming local customs to which we were introduced was the *luau*—a Hawaiian feast featuring a pig that's roasted underground with hot stones. The atmosphere was gay and colorful, with Hawaiian music and exotic rum drinks, but I didn't care too much for the roast pig. I've always liked pork chops, but I had a hard time adjusting to this autopsy cookout.

Another feature of the *luau* is a gooey substance called *poi*, which is allegedly beneficial for hangovers. *Poi,* it seems, is eaten with the fingers. I tried dipping into a blob of it, but had a hard time pulling my fingers back out. It had the consistency of instant quicksand and would be put to better use, it seems to me, making dental impressions.

Another authentic aspect of the *luau* was that everyone wore native costumes, such as *muu muus* and *lava lavas*. A *muu muu* is like a maternity dress for women who aren't pregnant. When a lady is wearing one it's hard to tell whether she's coming or going.

Although the Hawaiian girls are very graceful, and dance as though they have self-winding stomachs, a girl could do the hula in a *muu muu* and no one would ever know it. It's even difficult, when a girl is wearing one, to tell if she has a pretty figure. About all you can do is follow her until she hits sunlight.

Hawaii is famous for its informality of dress, and we spent some of the time dressed like beachcombers, but one of my sponsors decided, one night, that I should wear a dinner jacket on the show. I didn't mind the dinner jacket as much as the accompanying black bow tie. Trying to tie one of those frustrating strips of black obstinacy is like trying to wrap a package with a live serpent.

This night I popped out of the shower and, before getting dressed, began to practice. For some minutes I sat on the bed, barefoot up to my Adam's apple, tying and untying the tie to make sure I could get the bow to look right.

As I wrestled with it I began to feel a chill from the air-conditioner over the bed. Since I couldn't figure out how to turn it off, I decided to put a towel over it to cut down the cold air. It was quite high up so I put a footstool on the bed, climbed up and was stuffing a towel against the unit when a little Hawaiian maid popped in to turn down the bed.

There I was, with nothing on but a black bow tie, teetering on a footstool on top of the bed and waving a towel! Although I've spent most of my adult life ad-libbing, all I could think of to say in my embarrassing predicament was "Aloha."

23

The Sun Never Rises on the British Empire

SOME friends of mine flew to London not long ago with their two children. They landed in a heavy fog at the London airport and in just a matter of minutes were whisked into the terminal to wait for their luggage to come through customs. While they stood they noticed that their young daughter had darted to a desk and was hurriedly writing a postcard to her grandmother. Peering over her shoulder, they saw that she had written: "The contrast between England and the United States is amazing!"

Well, I've visited England several times, in and out of fogs, theirs and mine, and the contrast between England and the United States *is* amazing. That difference is the thing that makes England and the English so delightful. I've always loved the British and most things British, and have been a card-carrying Anglophile for years.

In fact, when I first arrived in Hollywood, under contract to R.K.O. Studios, one of the first things I did was to rush out and buy a sporty little red MG roadster. But I was so confused by the operating instructions, because of the British terms, like *bonnet* for hood and *fascia* for dashboard, that I had to phone David Niven to find out how to get it out of the garage.

The thing I admire about the British is their remarkable spirit, and it was displayed in various small but significant ways whenever we visited there. I was talking with one Englishman about our trip over and told him that with jets you could now fly from London to New York in six hours.

The Englishman cocked an eye at me and asked, "But *why?*"

The British attitude toward the world around them was also perfectly illustrated, I thought, by a headline I saw while there. HEAVY FOG. CONTINENT ISOLATED.

The weather is a problem in Britain, and it may be that the British have developed their stout, chin-up attitude just to be able to bear it. There is an old saying that the sun never sets on the British Empire, and there have been times while visiting there that I began to suspect it never *rises* on it either.

During one trip I heard this weather report on the radio— "Rain and fog. Continued fair."

To be quite fair, the English weather was often pleasant when we were there and I remember one trip when it was sunny and bright for two weeks, with the temperatures in the seventies. I must say, though, that the Londoners seemed to have some difficulty in adjusting to it. Several times I thought I saw them ducking into doorways until the sunlight passed over.

Everyone in London seems to carry umbrellas, but when it rains only the Americans open them. The British go so far as to put them inside their raincoats so they won't get wet.

I got a bowler and umbrella for strolling in London, but somehow they don't feel right on an American and the British don't take very kindly to our using them.

"An American wearing a bowler in London," one Englishman told me, "is like an Englishman turning up in America with a scalp at his belt."

Not only the weather but some of the customs, we found, took a bit of getting used to. The money, for instance, proved quite a puzzle to us, as it seems to many Americans. I finally got to understand shillings and pounds, but when they started talking about quid and bob they lost me.

At first, when the taxi driver named a sum I couldn't understand, I'd have him drive around until he reached an amount I *could* figure out. The British are extremely honest, but whenever I got change I had the uneasy feeling that someone was making money on me. Perhaps it was because anyone who made change for me always smiled when they counted it out.

London is a wonderful city for shopping, particularly for men, and I made several shopping forays to its great stores like Fortnum and Mason's, Harrods and the fine tailor shops along Savile Row. However, good as they are, British shops have their eccentricities.

On our last trip Peggy Cass discovered, after her arrival, that she had forgotten to bring toothpaste. Having arrived in London a few days ahead of her, I volunteered to lead her to a chemist's, as they call a drug store in England. After dinner that night I steered her to one near our hotel where she announced that she would like some toothpaste.

"Toothpaste is off, Modom," the clerk declared.

"But I see some," said Peggy, pointing to a shelf. "It's right there."

"I'm sorry, Modom," the clerk insisted. "We do not handle toilet requirements after six."

This threatened to touch off a full-fledged brawl. Peggy continued to demand toothpaste with a fervor that would have gladdened the heart of Procter and Gamble. The clerk stood firm with the same bulldog British spirit that repelled the Spanish Armada.

Peggy is a hot-tempered Boston Irish lass, and her dispute with the clerk seemed to be growing into the most violent Anglo-Irish hostilities since the Easter Uprising of 1916. I finally managed to lead Peggy away from the fray by assuring her that not only could she share my toothpaste, but that it contained hexachlorophene.

Just as some British customs were a puzzle to us, our television show, with its informality and cascade of commercials, must have been equally baffling to the English. The commercials, especially, seemed to confuse the British audiences, and some of them got more laughs than our jokes.

"He seems to be very funny for a salesman," one member of the audience whispered about me. "Coming to his show is like going to a bloomin' store."

I tried to explain American TV to the British audiences in terms they would understand. A late show like ours, I explained, would probably have kept Lady Chatterley at home, or at least have given the Lord something to do in the evenings. However, the British audience didn't seem to know quite how to take me and it occurred to me that this might have been because it was a shock to meet an American who wasn't in England to swim the English Channel.

I tried to establish rapport with the audience by telling them how much I admired the British and that, in fact, my family had *gone back* on the Mayflower. However, the audiences greeted me with an attitude that was either customary British reserve or just overwhelming indifference. Some audiences were warmer than others, of course. The more enthusiastic ones stared and said "Hmmmm."

One of the great joys of doing the show from England was having as guests some of the great British actors and talkers. The British excel as conversationalists and we had some of their finest, including Robert Morley, the great actor and wit, Bea Lillie, the titled comedienne who describes herself as "a Lady in her own wrong," Lord Robert Boothby, Michael Foote and Malcolm Muggeridge, the former editor of *Punch*. This urbane crew wrangled with each other, said outrageous things, insulted me and otherwise disported themselves, all in a proper British way, of course.

A vicar was being splashed over the London front pages the last time we were there, for carrying brotherly love a bit too far with his lady parishioners, and I remarked on the predilection for scandal in some British papers. Robert Morley, who has been playing Oscar Wilde almost as long and frequently as Lucy Monroe has been singing "The Star Spangled Banner," defended the British and charged that the Americans were not a passionate race.

"What do you mean, not passionate?" protested Peggy Cass. "We went from one boatload to 180 million people in three hundred years!"

As Morley fenced with Peggy, with an air of lofty tolerance, I said to him, "You're sort of a nice Malcolm Muggeridge."

"There's no such thing," observed Joyce Grenfell.

We also had quite a spirited discussion with our British guests over their food. I remarked that the British had invented penicillin but that they couldn't even make a good bowl of soup. "I had kippers this morning," I said, "and it was like eating a fat brush."

Again, however, Morley rushed stoutly to the defense of English cooking. "Your American food," he charged, "is over-described and undercooked."

After the show, Morley took Peggy and me to a fine London restaurant, where he announced to the maitre d'hotel that it was his birthday. We had a charming dinner, with lavish service, and the management sent a bottle of fine wine with the compliments of the house.

After the dinner I congratulated Robert again on his birthday. "It really isn't my birthday," he chuckled. "I always say it is when I go to a restaurant. They make such a fuss over you then."

I love hearing the English talk, not only for what they say but for their engaging manner of speaking. Even a few days in London convinces you of the wisdom of George Bernard Shaw's remark that the English and Americans are divided by a common language. Randy, who watches a number of TV shows made in England, had less trouble understanding the English accents than I did.

"They all talk like Robin Hood," she explained to me.

Even though some English accents are so English as to be almost unintelligible, I couldn't get over the suspicion that if you woke an Englishman in the middle of the night, he would talk just like an American.

Wilfred Hyde-White, the British actor, told me that English audiences like their actors unintelligible, and this curious trait seems to extend to all things British. I went to Berkeley Square with Randy, but the nightingales weren't singing. They were mumbling.

During our last visit to London, we stayed at the beautiful new Carlton Tower. This twenty-story hotel, the tallest in London, is as modern as our finest American hotels in most respects, but also reflects the conservatism of British tradition in little touches like the bridal suite which, I was told, is on two different floors.

One British friend advised us, on checking into the hotel, to ask the telephone operator to get Buckingham Palace and leave a message for the Queen to call me.

"She won't, of course," the friend said, "but you'll get great service at the hotel when the word gets around."

British hotels, like almost all European hotels, have superb service. One very European touch I liked was that you could put your shoes outside your door at night and get them back all nicely polished in the morning. In addition, by just walking down the corridor and noting the shoes you can tell a good deal about what's going on.

Outside one room I spotted two pair of women's shoes and a bowler. I never did understand *that* room. British hotels are very strict about any hanky-panky, however, although their house detectives are never overt. If a house detective sees a couple who he suspects are not married register, he simply orders tea for three sent up to their room and then joins them.

While in London we visited the various traditional places such as Buckingham Palace, the tower of London with its picturesque Beefeaters, Hyde Park with its uninhibited speakers and hecklers of every stripe, and Madame Tussaud's with its lifelike figures of everyone from Napoleon to Bob Hope. We also tried to see some of the lesser-known, out of the way places rarely visited by tourists. For instance, we visited Number 9 Downing Street. .

We had one pleasant surprise during our last visit. I got a chauffeur-driven car one day to take Miriam and Randy to lunch at a picturesque country inn out beyond Windsor Castle. While nearing the Castle, we saw a station wagon, with a lone woman driving, coming down a private road toward the main highway along which we were traveling. As the car stopped to wait for us to pass, I noticed that the woman driver, with a scarf over her head, looked somehow familiar.

"My God, it's the Queen!" our driver exclaimed.

Sure enough, it was Queen Elizabeth, driving alone in a dusty station wagon and looking like any other housewife bound for the local supermarket with the week's shopping list. Randy waved frantically and the Queen smiled as we passed.

"I wonder," I said to Randy, "how she knew we'd be passing just then?"

One of the most rewarding things about London is its flourishing theater, and going to shows there is always a stimulating adventure. There are about twice as many plays running in London as there are in New York, and it costs roughly half as much to see them.

Not all the shows are good, of course, and one night when I went with Hans Conreid, the actor, we encountered one which was quite dreary. We sat restlessly through the first act and waited impatiently for the intermission so we could escape into the night.

When the curtain finally came down, and the lights went up for the intermission, we headed for the door. In the aisle, however, we bumped into Raymond Massey, the distinguished actor, and his wife, whom we knew from the States.

They went out with us for a smoke and we had a pleasant chat through the brief intermission. Then, as the lights dimmed for the second act, and the Masseys started back in with the rest of the audience, I saw a chance to flee and whispered to Hans to join me in my getaway.

"That was a terrible thing to do," Hans said, as we headed back to our hotel. "I know the show was a bore, but it was very bad manners to walk out. What will the Masseys think?"

I too began having misgivings as Hans repeated gloomily all the way home, "I wish we hadn't done that. What will the Masseys think?"

A few days later, when I was just beginning to get over my remorse over what Hans had insisted was our breach of manners, I got a phone call from Raymond Massey.

"I've been trying for days to get you," he said. "I wanted to apologize for the other night. My wife and I couldn't stand the show, so we sneaked out right after talking with you. She's been nagging me ever since about our bad manners. She keeps saying, 'What will Jack Paar and Hans Conreid think?' I hope you don't think we were rude!"

One thing about London that startles most Americans is the British press.

At its best, it is equal or superior to our best papers, but at its worst it is even worse than our worst, if such a thing is possible. Some of the British papers seem like nothing more nor less than trade journals for sex maniacs.

The worst segment of the British press takes a special delight in needling American entertainers and, since I've had my hands full with the U.S. press, I stayed discreetly out of their way while in Britain.

One of the biggest papers in London, or in the world, is Lord Beaverbrook's *Daily Express* with a circulation of over 4,250,000. On my first trip to England I was invited by Lord Beaverbrook to have dinner at his country estate in Surrey, about an hour outside London. The evening with the lively gnomelike Canadian-born publisher was a highlight of our visit.

He had a number of prominent guests, including Lady Dunn, Lord and Lady Balfour and Michael Foote, an outspoken, controversial member of the British Parliament. Since both the waspish Lord Beaverbrook and the blunt-spoken Foote take delight in needling many things American, some acidulous conversation crackled around the dinner table. At times I was tempted to try to pass for a southern Canadian.

After dinner, as we were chatting, Lady Dunn announced, "Mr. Paar, I hear you're a genius. Say something funny."

Most performers loath that challenge, and usually ignore it, but considering the company I thought I'd better try to rise to the occasion. I said that I was in England as part of our cultural exchange for Brendan Behan, and tried my best to make a few amusing comments on the difference in American and British customs and attitudes.

I explained that I had always felt a special fondness for the British and that one of my great, great grandfathers had deserted at Valley Forge. I commented on the British love of tradition and old monuments and told how one man tried to get me to take an hour's drive just to see an eighty-year-old Coca-Cola sign.

As I tossed off my little sallies, I was getting no great reaction from the guests. Lady Dunn looked particularly bleak. Still I plunged valiantly on, determined to wring a laugh from my little audience.

I mentioned the British fondness for titles. We didn't have that sort of thing in America, I reminded them, although we did elevate Elvis Presley to sergeant. This drew a slight smile from one of my titled listeners. The reason Americans don't have customs like being knighted, I explained, is that you couldn't get anybody to kneel down in front of someone holding a sword.

I teased them about the difficulty of understanding English as spoken by the English. "This morning I was gargling in my hotel bathroom," I said, "and a maid said it was the funniest story she had heard in a long time."

I admitted that I was making rapid headway in learning to understand the language as they spoke it, though, and said that I had already been able to let my interpreter go. A look around the table still revealed no smiles, so I decided that my efforts to be funny at this command performance were a flop.

"You don't seem very fond of the British," Lady Dunn remarked, as I sputtered to a stop.

"To the contrary, I love the British," I said. "Who else sent a Hallmark card when you lost India?"

At that, Lady Dunn and the rest of the distinguished guests finally all roared with laughter. The whole experience left me a little baffled by the British sense of humor, although I now understand the Boston Tea Party better.

24

The Italian National Pastime

IN ITALY, we discovered, the favorite spectator sport is girl-watching. While in Rome we tried to follow the old adage to do as the Romans do, but it wasn't easy. Like the rest of the tourists, we spent most of our time looking at the churches and ruins, while the Romans were all looking at the tourists, particularly if they were female.

"The Italian male has a way of looking at any reasonably attractive female as if she were the first woman he'd ever seen in his life," Mary Chamberlain, an American writer-friend, explained to us. "His eyes take on an expression of stunned wonder, and zigzag from her head to her toes, as he makes a mental relief map of the rolling crests and hidden valleys of this new and unexplored continent."

The Italian men do more, I quickly learned, than simply gaze enraptured at passing women, especially Americans. "The Italians have a very bad attitude toward women," one American in Rome warned me. "They pinch them."

"The worst part of it is," another American added, "that the women like it."

The Italians seem to feel nothing amiss in playfully pinching the derriere of a strange woman on the street, and even consider it a mark of admiration to bestow such a playful tweak.

American girls are not as prone to accept a pinch from a strange man as a tribute, and have some difficulty adjusting to the Italian outlook. Irving R. Levine, N.B.C.'s Rome correspondent, who with his attractive wife Nancy briefed us on

Italian customs, told us of one American woman who complained indignantly to an Italian policeman that a man had pinched her.

The policeman asked her to point out the man. She did, and the policeman shrugged, "It's okay. I know him. He's all right."

Peggy Cass, who was with us in Rome, was insulted because no man tried to pinch her.

"They were very friendly in other ways, though," Peggy admitted. She said that workers on the street sometimes raise their glasses and say, *"Bella ragazza, bella ragazza."*

"I think it means 'pretty girl,' " Peggy said. "I guess it's the next best thing to being pinched."

With Miriam and Randy along, there was no opportunity of my participating in Rome's favorite outdoor sport. We spent our time sedately visiting the Colosseum, the Forum and other historical sights of the Eternal City, as well as watching the ever-changing scene on the Spanish Steps below the Hassler Hotel where we stayed.

We also visited the Catacombs, the underground burial grounds of the early Christians. There are many of these under the streets of Rome and, while of great historical interest, the cramped, dark tunnels are no place for anyone with claustrophobia.

Knowing that I'm allergic to close quarters, and even get panicky driving through Rhode Island, Miriam looked doubtfully at the forbidding-looking entrance to the old burial chambers and asked our guide solicitously, "Do you have any *short* catacombs?"

We explored catacombs long and short, however, and visited St. Peter's and the other magnificent old churches of Rome. We were joined on these sight-seeing jaunts by Charley Weaver, who is something of a student of antiquity, particularly in Scotch.

Finally, footsore and weary from visiting so many churches,

Charley sent a postcard to a Catholic friend saying, "I can't find a Masonic Temple here."

Peggy Cass, who is a Catholic, had an audience with the Pope while we were in Rome. Vatican etiquette requires that women received by the Pontiff wear conservative black dresses with high necklines and long sleeves, and Peggy was in a swivet about whether the dress she had would be proper for the occasion.

After days of fretting over what she would wear for the audience, Peggy finally sighed, "Maybe it would be better if they just blindfolded the Pope!"

In our exploration of Rome, we admired the magnificent Sistine Chapel, strolled along the Via Veneto, sat in the sun in front of Doney's sipping campari and soda and watching the Italians watch us. We also gorged on *fettucine* at Alfredo's and tossed coins into the Fountain of Trevi.

Charley Weaver accompanies us on most of these peregrinations but he balked at going to the Fountain of Trevi. Charley, the last of the big-time savers, recoiled from the idea of throwing coins into a fountain because of the legend that it would someday bring you back to Rome.

The most striking thing to us was the contrast between the old and the new in the beautiful city which dates back beyond the Caesars. It was a startling sight to see people, even nuns and monks, rushing about on Vespa motor scooters past ancient ruins like the Colosseum or the Baths of Caracalla. The Italians whip about with gleeful abandon on their Vespas, seemingly thriving on the din they create.

They apparently consider any pedestrian fair game and are said to pursue hapless pedestrians onto the sidewalk and even amid the tables of sidewalk cafés. The scooter riders almost all wear sunglasses and wide smiles as they dart recklessly about, and Rome is the only city I know where you can find people with bugs on their teeth.

Italian drivers are dedicated to both noise and speed, and

if there's anything an Italian enjoys as much as a pretty girl it's a good loud automobile accident. Ever since chariot races and feeding Christians to the lions went out of style in Rome, such accidents have become a popular substitute because witnesses all join in the ensuing dispute over whose fault the collision was. Even a slight altercation between a motor scooter and a pushcart will bring accident *aficionados* from blocks around, all eager to plunge into the fray.

We had a vivid example of the Italian fondness for traffic disputes when we visited the Fountain of Trevi. While Miriam and Randy and I were gazing at the beautiful fountain, our chauffeur, a dark, voluble man named Renzo, apparently violated some minor traffic regulation by parking nearby.

A policeman, in blue uniform and crested helmet, came up and began arguing with him. Renzo argued back furiously, waving his arms expressively. As the rising sound of voices reached us, we hurried back toward our car, where Renzo and the policeman were still disputing passionately—sneering, shrugging and threatening.

A crowd began to gather, obviously delighted by the ruckus. As the dispute grew in violence, spectators began to join happily in the argument, and vendors began drifting up to sell Coca-Colas and pizzas to the noncombatants. The crowd continued to grow as more spectators appeared, gesturing wildly and squabbling fiercely.

Finally Renzo broke off the engagement and stalked off huffily to a telephone to call his superiors. Outraged, the policeman marched majestically to another phone to call *his* superiors.

Awed by the whole conflict, which we had innocently started, we quietly sneaked off through the crowd, leaving the field to the witnesses, several of whom were still arguing vehemently.

Another idiosyncrasy of the Italians is their hotel bookkeeping system. We might be told, for instance, that the daily rate for our hotel suite was the *lire* equivalent of $25 a day. Yet, when I'd get the bill, it would be roughly double that. The answer lies in a little booby-trap called extras.

They make a formidable list. Every Italian hotel bill has a service charge of from 15 to 20 percent of the total. Then there's a charge of around a dollar a day for central heating. I must say I didn't particularly notice the heat, but there it was on the bill. At some hotels there is even a visitor's tax. In addition, there is another little surcharge known as the General Revenue Tax, amounting to two percent of the bill.

If you order food in your room, there's a ten percent tax on that. If you order food or drink at the bar, the tax is six to eight percent. Finally, when you pay the grand total, the cashier affixes to the receipt a small and very official-looking government stamp, which looks rather like a postage stamp.

This is your official notice that your bill is paid. Then, as a final gesture, they charge you for the stamp!

No doubt about it, the Italians don't do things the way other people do. Therein, I imagine, lies much of their special charm.

After Rome we visited Venice—one of the most unique and beautiful cities in the world. For years I had heard conflicting opinions about this ancient city which is not only on but practically in the Adriatic. Some travelers had told me it was the most beautiful city in the world. But George Jessel cautioned me, "Venice is like your Aunt Agatha. You should think of her, and tell people how nice she is, but never visit her!"

But when we cast eyes on Venice at last, I was delighted. The whole city looked like a set for an Esther Williams picture. It's an amazing city, built on 122 islands, with 444 gondolas, 500 bridges and, seemingly, 10,000 baritones.

As I looked out over the city of canals from our beautiful suite in the Gritti Palace Hotel, once the home of a fifteenth century Doge, I was reminded of Robert Benchley's cable to a friend, on arriving in Venice: "Please advise. Streets full of water."

It's wonderful to glide through the canals in a gondola, far from the noisy motor scooters of Rome. The only way you can commit a traffic violation in Venice is by jay-swimming. Together with Charley Weaver and his son Mike, we explored the city by gondola, fed the pigeons in St. Mark's Square and did all the things that have enchanted tourists for centuries.

In St. Mark's Square we saw Desdemona and Othello strike the gong in the ancient bell tower. We strolled the Merceria with its hundreds of shops and saw the house where Napoleon lived, where Verdi composed *Rigoletto* and where Browning and Wagner died. We sampled chicken on a bed of *fettuccine* and exotic sea delicacies like octopus salad and sea snails.

Venice has beautiful leather goods and women's clothes, and Miriam and Randy had quite a time for themselves shopping. We passed one shop that had some chic dresses in the window, so Miriam and Randy went in to look at them while I waited outside watching the gondolas go by.

Miriam doesn't speak Italian and through the window I could see her trying to make herself understood with gestures. She pointed at different dresses she liked and gesticulated to indicate sizes. Several times I saw her try to pick a dress off a rack, and each time the Italian owner kept pulling them away from her and angrily expostulating.

Finally, a man in the back of the place, who spoke some English, noticed the rumpus and rushed in to quell the tug-o-war.

"Modom," he explained with a smile. "Zis is a dry-cleaning chop."

From Venice, we flew by Alitalia Airlines to Nice on the French Riviera, where we got a parting demonstration of what dedicated girl-watchers Italian males are.

We had a half dozen bags, which required some strenuous

juggling, and while I wrestled to get them checked aboard I got not even a passing glance from the Italian pilots standing nearby. The pilots were too deeply engrossed in flirting with some Spanish girls, who were also waiting to board the flight.

The Italians were a debonair lot, with dark wavy hair and flashing smiles, and were much more interested in the girls than in whether our luggage ever got aboard. Finally the girls boarded the plane, closely followed by the Italian crew, and we took off for Nice.

Later, when I got back on the show, I told about the incident and registered a tongue-in-cheek complaint about the amorous Italian aeronauts. A day or two later I got this letter to use on any future flights on Alitalia Airlines:

To all Alitalia employees: *Buon Giorno!*

This is to introduce Signor Jack Paar of New York.

Whenever Signor Paar appears at an Alitalia office, will you please release one man from girl-watching long enough to handle his baggage?

Signor Paar is a very important man in American television.

You should also know he is a good friend of Guido Panzini!

Grazie molto! Distinti Saluti!

25

The Last Bullfight of El Chicken

WHEN we visited Spain I got to indulge in one of my suppressed desires. I went to a bullfight and rooted for the bull. Being in show business I know what it is to have someone plunging knives in your back, and I'm allergic to this kind of carrying on, even if it's a picador or matador sticking *banderillas* into a bull.

For years I've read Hemingway and Barnaby Conrad and other exponents of the hairy-chested school of writing. They profess to find something fascinating and dramatic in bullfighting, but it holds no charms for me and I wouldn't know an *aficionado* from an avocado. I know it's supposed to be a fair contest between man and bull, but as Bob Considine once remarked, you see more old bullfighters around than you do old bulls.

I never like to see anything fixed, except traffic tickets, and the spectacle is even less inviting if the victim is a brave bull. If the Spanish want to have fights where the victim is doomed from the start, it seems to me they should use something like Volkswagens, and not strong and noble animals.

We didn't plan to attend a bullfight while in Spain, and detoured the famed festival at Pamplona, where the bulls chase the people through the streets in what is a sort of Spanish version of our subway rush hour. However, about the time we visited Spain, there were a series of incidents in which bulls routed their tormentors. I felt, with a little encouragement and some organized cheering, the bulls might reverse the whole trend of things.

At San Sebastian de los Reyes, one bull sent three matadors to the hospital in a single day. In the town of Almoradi, a matador dispatched a bull with a clean thrust—or so he thought. He was strutting around the ring to the cries of *"Olé!"* when the supposedly dead bull suddenly revived. Lumbering to its feet, the wounded animal took out after the startled matador who probably set a new Spanish sprint record in his haste to get behind the barrier. He beat the bull in a photo finish.

Word was getting around among the matadors that the bulls were staging a rally, and the bullfighters were understandably a little nervous. At Majorca, a young matador named Pepe Nunez watched the bull he was to fight maul the other two matadors on the program and wisely decided he wanted no part of this ill-tempered animal. He hid behind the barrier, announcing his unconditional surrender, until the police hauled him off to the pokey.

With the bulls making a comeback, I decided to lend a little moral support. So I took Miriam and Randy to a bullfight while we were in Madrid. Charley Weaver had heard that they served wine in skins, so he and his son Mike came along.

I must say there was a certain color and excitement to the spectacle. The matadors marched across the arena, the sun glistening against the gold sequins on their costumes, followed by their banderillos and mounted picadors. Then the trumpets blared and the bull charged into the ring to meet the first matador.

"Olé," the crowd roared, as the matador eluded the rushing bull, performing a series of veronica passes with his cape.

I stood up and yelled, "Boo!"

The Spanish people around me looked surprised. I think they thought I had yelled "Moo," and that I was trying to confuse the bull. Miriam and Randy were busy pretending they weren't with me. Charley was occupied with his wineskin.

Next the picadors, on padded horses, thrust with their long lances at the great muscle behind the bull's neck. The bull charged one picador, putting him to flight.

"*Olé!*" I yelled, on behalf of the bull.

We watched while the matadors killed two bulls, and I booed the bullfighters and yelled "*Olé*" for the bulls. By then I had had enough and I gathered, from the looks of the crowd around us, that they were getting a little tired of my unorthodox cheering.

Miriam and Randy were happy to leave, too, and Charley cheerfully agreed to come when we said he could bring his wineskin with him.

Despite my dim views on bullfighting, I agreed to fight a bull as a joke while we were in Madrid. Not a real bull, of course, but the next thing to one—a cow.

The way this came about was that someone suggested it would make a great spot for my show if I were to stage a mock bullfight and film it. I had misgivings about the whole idea. In the first place, I pointed out, I didn't like bullfighting. Secondly, I particularly didn't like it if *I* was doing the fighting.

However, Charley Weaver and Paul Keyes finally talked me into it. They pointed out that Ava Gardner and even Elsa Maxwell had fought bulls. At that I announced my willingness to die, if necessary, for N.B.C., my agents and the Nielsen rating system.

The bullfight took place at a *finca,* or ranch, outside Madrid. I came out dressed—if not armed—to the teeth. In a sequined jacket, tight toreador pants, knee stockings and slippers, I looked like a refugee from a Rudolph Valentino movie.

Glancing around the ring I saw the animal I was to face. I had been promised a nice docile cow, but this beast was acting strangely warlike. It was in the clutches of several handlers, who were having a tough time hanging on to it.

It seemed unfair for my opponent to have several handlers,

while I had no one in my corner except Charley Weaver, who was discreetly hiding behind the barrier. Miriam was in the stands, but she was holding her hands over her eyes, and I could see Randy's lips moving in prayer.

As I strode toward the animal, my suspicions became aroused. I had specified clearly that I didn't want to fight anything I couldn't milk, and this animal was showing signs of hostility not usually found in cows. I began to get the feeling that some fun-loving soul had slipped me a ringer, a genuine bull, and a mean one at that. I thought of Belmonte and Manolete, and I began to feel very el chicken.

Then they turned the animal loose. I strode dubiously toward it, eyeing the beast carefully. Without being indelicate, I was trying to see whether it had the equipment which distinguishes cows from bulls. The animal trotting toward me looked downright fierce.

I remembered the skimpy cape I was carrying, and suddenly felt as helplessly exposed as Brigitte Bardot in a hand towel. I waved the cape, the way I had seen Rudolph Valentino do it in the movies, but it was like waving an engraved invitation. The beast was coming on at a fast trot and was obviously in no mood for games. This, I suddenly realized *is* the moment of truth! And the truth was, I could plainly see, that I was fighting a real bull!

I did the only courteous thing I knew. I left. Turning tail, I lit out for the barrier.

"Use your cape, Johnny!" I heard Charley Weaver yell.

I didn't bother to look back, but I could tell from the clatter of hooves that the bull was closing in fast. I made a flying leap for the barrier, one jump ahead of the bull, and knocked out all my wind.

Later, at the hotel, the doctor said that two of my ribs were just badly bruised—not broken—and that I'd be all right in a couple of days. That was my first and last bullfight or, as Miriam called it, bullflight.

The result, as scored by *Time* magazine: no ears, no tail, no hoofs, two bruised ribs.

One of our most interesting experiences in Spain, after my retirement from the bull ring, was watching the filming of Samuel Bronston's five-million-dollar epic, *King of Kings*. Bronston had previously filmed *John Paul Jones,* the story of the American naval hero, in Spain, and the picture was shelled so heavily by the critics it became known in movie circles as John Paul Jones' only defeat.

But Bronston showed no wounds from his disastrous naval engagement when we met him and graciously showed us around the set, where we encountered St. John the Baptist drinking a Coca-Cola and Mary Magdalene in sun glasses.

He and director Nicholas Ray let Randy play the role of one of the children welcoming Christ, played by Jeffrey Hunter, to Jerusalem. Bronston even let me ride a camel, a dreary, ill-tempered animal that looks like a horse which has been put together by a committee.

With my luck, I managed to get one with a mean disposition and a sharp hump. I have never been particularly fond of either camels or actors, and to meet a camel who was also an actor didn't improve my opinion of either. Also, although Bronston was spending five million dollars on the picture, he was economizing on little things and using camels with only one hump.

However, it was interesting to watch the making of the picture, which involved thousands of extras from the Spanish Army. Playing Jews of more than two thousand years ago was easy for the Spanish soldiers, who have been in more movies than wars lately. In fact, in recent years the Spanish soldiers have turned up in pictures as Romans, Crusaders, Tartars and Turks. If it goes much further, when a soldier enlists in the Spanish Army he'll take an oath of allegiance not to Generalissimo Franco but to the Hollywood Screen Actors' Guild.

We were on hand the day they filmed the Sermon on the

Mount, with seventy-five hundred Spanish actors on the hillside.

"This scene will be the first in which all the actors see Hunter in the character of Christ," director Ray told us.

Five cameras were running as the handsome young actor, dressed in white, came forward to the edge of the mount. As he did, most of the thousands of extras dropped spontaneously to their knees and crossed themselves. It was an awe-inspiring moment, one of the most touching scenes I have ever watched.

Later, however, Ray and Bronston learned that the practice of making the sign of the cross didn't come into existence until some years after Christ died, so the whole vast, gripping scene had to be filmed again.

While the movie was being made the picture's press agent sent out a story saying that Bronston was keeping the plot a secret.

A newspaperman called the press agent and asked what the release meant. "Mr. Bronston doesn't want the plot revealed," the press agent said.

"Well, I know a book that has the plot in it," the newspaperman declared. "It's called the New Testament."

"For gosh sake," the press agent implored, "don't tell the producer!"

26

Easter in the Holy Land

IT WAS a dark, overcast, misty Good Friday in Jerusalem as Miriam, Randy and I stood reverently watching the thousands of cross-bearing pilgrims from many lands trudging along the Via Doloroso—the sad road trod by Jesus centuries ago. At three o'clock—the traditional hour of His death on the cross —the peal of bells began sounding in the many churches of the sadly divided ancient city. Almost at the exact moment when, twenty centuries ago, the heavens had darkened and the curtain of the Temple had been rent, the grey skies opened and the sun burst through, flooding the moving scene with an almost unearthly light.

This dramatic quirk of nature, bathing the old, cobbled, rain-washed road and the plodding pilgrims in a sudden glow of yellow sunlight, was one of the most memorable moments of an eventful visit to the Holy Land at the Easter season in 1961.

Only in the Holy Land, to paraphrase my friend Harry Golden, could an American Protestant attend a Catholic Mass in the morning, have lunch with a Moslem in the old city of Jerusalem in Jordan and dine that evening with Jewish friends in the vital, busy new nation of Israel.

That swift juxtaposition of events in one single day seemed to symbolize the amazing contrast of the old and the new— the serenity and yet the danger—in the land where Christ once lived and taught. It was a moving yet often troubling experience to walk amid the very surroundings made holy by the

Man of Peace, yet to know that Jerusalem was harshly divided between Arab Jordan and Jewish Israel.

Yet even barbed-wire and armed guards could not detract from our feeling of wonder at the sites made so familiar by the Scriptures, and of sharing these unforgettable experiences with our only child.

Led by a pleasant Arab guide named Moses Taha, we visited the garden of Gethsemane where Jesus prayed, the Potter's Field purchased with the thirty pieces of silver hurled away by a despairing Judas, and Calvary where Christ was crucified. But the most real and moving place to me was the site of the Palace of Caiaphas, the High Priest, where Jesus spent his last night on earth.

The Roman Catholic Church of St. Peter now stands on the site, but we were able to go under it, where excavations have uncovered the very spot where Christ was tried, condemned, mocked and imprisoned the day before his crucifixion.

We went down a dark passageway below the church to the courtyard where Peter denied Christ and the cell, hewn from rock, where Jesus was cast to await execution. As we peered into the dark cell, our priest guide suddenly threw a beam from his flashlight into the cell and said, "Look at the wall."

There, faintly visible in the rock, was a startling natural outline that looked like a kneeling figure. The sudden sight of this phenomenon in the ancient rock gave the strange feeling of being transported, in an instant, back through the centuries to the very night when Jesus was confined in the cell into which we now peered.

At each of these scenes, holy to Christians, the ancient and revered were harshly blended with the crass and modern. We visited sites so holy that we unconsciously lowered our voices to a whisper, yet all around us was the hubbub of Arab life with its exotic smells, the babble of bargaining merchants and the strange wail of Arabic music on the radio. In Pilate's courtyard, where Jesus was sentenced to death, a dark-eyed little Arab urchin played stickball, alone.

Crossing from the old city of Jerusalem in Jordan, through the Mandelbaum Gate into the new country of Israel, is a strange experience. We walked along an ancient cobbled street, between machine-gun emplacements and armed sentries, across the fifty-year No Man's Land separating the two countries. An Arab youngster carried our bags to the midway point in the heavily guarded sector, then an Israeli youngster met us there to carry them the rest of the way.

In Israel, as in Jordan, we found the same sharp contrast of ancient and modern, yet in a vastly different culture. In Bethlehem, five miles south of Jerusalem, we saw the cave where the Christ child was born, the site of the temple where He worshipped as a child and the well where Mary drew water, looking much as it must have then. Almost all of these shrines of Christendom were surrounded by Moslem merchants, selling bibles, rosaries and holy medals.

After exploring Jerusalem and Bethlehem, we took a small plane and flew over the hills where the shepherds tended their flocks, over the Negev, the breathtakingly beautiful but barren desert, and over green *Kibbutzim,* and new collective settlements where everyone works and shares in the rewards. Our plane landed at Tiberius, on the Sea of Galilee, near Capernaum and the beautiful ruins of a temple where Jesus once preached, and the hill, overlooking the sea, where He gave the Sermon on the Mount.

From these ancient and impressive scenes we flew back to modern Tel Aviv, a bustling new city, where non-stop jets come shrieking in from New York. There we stayed at the Sheraton Tel Aviv, a spanking new two-hundred-room hotel, on a bluff overlooking the glittering Mediterranean. Although the new hotel, built of limestone quarried in Nazareth, is as modern as any hotel in the United States, it was having a few little problems during our stay there shortly after it opened.

Miriam called to confirm our return airline reservations but had difficulty making herself understood. Several times I heard her repeat the word "confirm" which the person at the other end of the wire seemed not to understand.

I finally solved the whole thing. "Just tell him to Bar Mitzvah the tickets," I advised Miriam. That did the trick.

The Israelis are justly proud of what their little nation has accomplished in thirteen years, and they took obvious pleasure in showing us around thriving Tel Aviv. Among the handsome buildings we were shown was the beautiful new Mann Auditorium.

Seeing it recalled an amusing story I had heard about the auditorium when I interviewed Mayor Willy Brandt of West Berlin not long before. When he had visited Tel Aviv and been shown Mann Auditorium, Brandt praised Israel's conciliatory gesture in naming it after the late German author, Thomas Mann.

But the auditorium was not named after the German author, it was explained to Brandt, but after Fredrick R. Mann, of Philadelphia.

"What did he write?" the puzzled Mayor asked.

"A check," was the reply.

We were also shown Israel's first golf course, at Caesarea, an ancient Roman seaport founded by Herod. The rolling eighteen-hole private course is bounded on one side by the Mediterranean and on the other by hostile Jordan.

"If you slice the ball you go into the ocean," complained Art Buchwald. "If you hook it, you could start a war. If you hit an Arab, the United Nations penalizes you two strokes."

Golfers are reported to have unearthed old Roman coins blasting out of sand traps, and an old civilization is being dramatically unearthed all around Caesarea even as the new one rises. Along the beach, where we watched tourists splashing and sun bathing, is an ancient aqueduct lately dug from under the sands of centuries and nearby a magnificent marble Roman theater, also recently unearthed.

The whole effect of the mixture of Christian landmarks and relics of ancient Jewish and Roman culture, with the bustle of the emerging young nation of Israel, made a fascinating kaleidscope. One minute we might be gazing on some scene associated with the life of Christ, or a monument built by the Romans, and the next we would find ourselves sitting in a luxurious, air-conditioned hotel, discussing Marilyn Monroe or the latest Broadway joke.

Israel is a melting pot of dozens of nationalities and languages, but there are so many Americans there that at times it seemed like a kosher New Jersey. I got the feeling I was back sitting around the Stage Delicatessen, eating knishes and pastrami with Max Asnas, Jack E. Leonard or Joey Bishop.

Tourism is the second largest industry, one official told me, adding with a twinkle in his eye that the first is bragging. It struck me that the little nation's biggest export might well be humor, for it seems to have wit and good spirits to spare. I found jokes and laughter on every hand in Israel, and the humor, much of it directed at themselves, stands the Israelis in good stead, hemmed in as they are on every hand by hostile Arab neighbors.

One story I heard in Tel Aviv was about the time when Greece suffered from an earthquake and the British sent in ships with food and medical supplies. Israel also sent a ship with supplies for the victims. In the Greek harbor one night, a British ship saw the little Israeli vessel dimly through the darkness.

"Ahoy, who are you?" the British captain hailed.

"Israeli," replied the Jewish ship.

"Who?" shouted the British captain through the darkness.

"Israeli," was the reply. "You may remember us as Palestine!"

"Oh, yes," was the British answer. "Are you still having trouble with the Jews?"

We came to Israel after brief visits in Egypt and Jordan—two of Israel's unfriendly Arab neighbors. Egypt seemed none too fond of Americans, either, and the streets near the Nile Hilton where we stayed in Cairo, were plastered with signs proclaiming—"Death to the murderers of Lumumba."

Egyptian officials were hospitable, however, and arranged for us to see some of Egypt's most famous sights. We visited the Sphinx and pyramids, which we could see from our hotel room, dined on a houseboat on the Nile and flew up that storied stream to Luxor, site of magnificent ruins, and Aswan where Russian engineers were directing the building of a giant dam dwarfing the pyramids in size.

I shot some films of the work on the great dam and the Egyptian government kindly sent along a lighting man, burdened down with lights, to assist me in the filming. I appreciated the gesture, but if there's one thing you don't need under the blazing sun in the Sahara desert it's more light. Also, there's another problem about photographic lights in the Sahara—there's no place to plug them in!

Our trip to the Middle East wound up spectacularly with a flying visit to Greece—literally. Our time was short and the Greek government graciously provided us with a helicopter, in which we flew over Athens for a unique and stunning view of that magnificent city. Strapped to the floor of the helicopter, which Randy referred to as the "teleprompter," we hovered over such glorious ruins as the Parthenon atop the Acropolis, the Temple of Apollo crowning Mt. Parnassus and the haunts of the Delphic Oracle, the Dorothy Kilgallen of ancient times.

The gleaming white ruins, the piercing blue skies and the azure water of the harbor, with the U.S. Sixth Fleet riding at anchor, formed an unforgettable picture. At the foot of the

Acropolis we wandered through the theater of Dionysus, where the plays of Aristophanes, Sophocles and Aeschylus were first performed, and the theater of Herodes Atticus, where they are still being played.

In addition to exploring the beautiful ruins, by helicopter and foot, we lazed along the waterfront at Piraeus, and sampled such Greek delicacies as vine leaves stuffed with rice and meat, stuffed artichokes and octopus. We even tried the Greek *retsina*—a wine laced with resin—a drinking sensation like gulping lighter fluid.

Our hosts in Athens were Mr. and Mrs. Louis Hepp, the N.B.C. correspondent and his wife, and a hospitable couple they were. They have a charming house which, like so many homes in Greece, utilizes a great deal of the beautiful marble so plentiful in that country.

Mrs. Hepp showed us around her house with its marble basins, marble tub, marble-topped kitchen table and marble fixtures, and murmured rather apologetically, "We can't afford Formica."

27

Instant Incident in Berlin

I SEEM to have stirred up more than my share of uproars in
my day. However, it wasn't until I took our show to Berlin
that I managed to create an *international* incident. In international blowups, as in the domestic variety, I discovered,
the fallout often far exceeds the explosion.

My instant incident erupted in September of 1961, when
I went to Berlin to telecast our program from that troubled
city just after the Soviet-sponsored East German government
slammed shut the border that divides East and West Berlin.
We filmed one hour of the program at the border of the American sector at Friedrichstrasse, showing the newly erected wall
and other points of interest on both sides of the border. We
also interviewed a few United States soldiers.

Overnight, the appearance of American soldiers on the
show set off a chain reaction flap that reached all the way
to Washington.

Members of Congress called the incident *shocking* and
intolerable. The White House was reportedly disturbed. The
State Department was upset. The Army took disciplinary action against the two officers who had assisted us. Lt. Col.
Dallas Hoadley, the information officer in Berlin was relieved
for "improper performance of duties," and Col. John Deane
Jr. was admonished for showing "poor judgment." The Hearst
papers denounced *"massed troops and armor"* at the border,
and the Communist East German *Neues Deutschland* said
darkly that we had *"staged war games"* and *"provocations."*

All this before anyone had seen the program in question!

What touched off the international uproar? What really happened to create such a far-reaching clamor? The truth is that the whole story was blown up out of all proportion and was the biggest exaggeration to come out of Germany since Baron Munchausen was operating there. As is often the case, the whole crazy chain of events was started by one distorted newspaper story.

It began:

"Fifty American soldiers yesterday moved rapidly down the rain-spattered street, and took possession of buildings overlooking the East-West Berlin border.

"A jeep mounting a 106 mm, recoilless anti-tank gun and others mounting machine guns went into position at the Friedrichstrasse crossing.

"One jeep with machine gun had a front wheel planted on the white stripe that indicates the border.

"Two Colonels arrived.

"The situation looked grim.

"It was the biggest turn-out the American Army had yet made along the wall that divides Communist from Free Berlin —and it was all for Jack Paar."

That story—written by one anonymous reporter and relayed back to the United States by United Press International —touched off an explosion in the capital, and no wonder! Without bothering to check the facts, Washington officials began to raise the Capitol roof.

Assistant Secretary of Defense Arthur Sylvester called the incident "disgraceful." Senate Majority Leader Mike Mansfield said the Berlin situation "was not a television spectacular to be made into some kind of game for the personal profit of personalities in the entertainment world," and Senator Saltonstall claimed it "might have led to a shooting scene." It took eleven columns in the *Congressional Record* to chronicle the senatorial fulminations over the imaginary "incident." And all based on one inaccurate newspaper story.

About the only members of Congress who weren't registering indignation over me were twelve junketing Congressmen who were in Rome. They were waxing indignant over having been stood up by actress Elizabeth Taylor on a movie set. While the Senators in Washington were demanding to know what I was doing in Berlin at a time of crisis, I couldn't help wondering what the junketing Congressmen were doing visiting a movie set in Rome. At least I was observing Berlin's cleavage, and not Elizabeth Taylor's. Also, at the same time that the Senators were criticizing the Army for cooperating with an entertainer in Berlin, some of them were cooperating with Hollywood by appearing in the movie *Advise and Consent* being filmed in the capital.

The newspapers and magazines added to the general hubbub by taking the highly exaggerated original story and further distorting the distortions. While the original U.P.I. story mentioned 50 soldiers and two jeeps with me at the border, *Newsweek* managed to boost it to 80 soldiers and seven jeeps.

For the record, here are the true facts behind the phantom Berlin "incident." Because of the tremendous interest sparked by the crisis there, I decided to take the show over and give our viewers a picture of what was happening. Where news and commentary programs were already exploring the military and political aspects of developments, I hoped, through a more informal approach, to show the human side of what was taking place.

The Army offered us their cooperation, just as they did to other American TV shows in Berlin. As a matter of fact, two other programs—N.B.C.'s *Here and Now* and C.B.S.'s *Eyewitness to History*—were both filming at the Friedrichstrasse border at the very time of the alleged "incident."

This kind of cooperation by the military is commonplace. At the same time that I was filming a handful of G.I.'s for an hour, 1600 marines and 22 ships of the U.S. Sixth Fleet were performing for Darryl Zanuck, who was shooting a movie about D-Day! Also, the Army ordered 700 soldiers from

Germany to France to support rock and roll singers Fabian, Paul Anka and other Hollywood heroes in the same picture.

The extent to which the military cooperates with entertainers is perhaps illustrated by a joke told me by Joey Bishop.

"Bob Hope was going to Greenland to entertain at Christmas but they found out there was only one sergeant and a private stationed there," he said. "They had to fly 10,000 men up from Fort Dix to be entertained so Bob's feelings wouldn't be hurt."

Our request in Berlin was very simple. I wanted to interview Col. John Deane, Jr., a much decorated officer, and asked him to bring along one or two other soldiers so that Peggy Cass and I could talk with them.

As it turned out he brought a squad of 12 men, explaining that he didn't want to single out some and leave others behind. I also asked for a jeep, to have something to sit on during the interview. That was the extent of it.

There happened to be an operational changeover of units while we were preparing to shoot, which accounted for more military personnel being at the border than normally. Also, a few off-duty officers had drifted up out of curiosity to watch the goings-on. The blown-up U.P.I. story made it sound as if the Army had restaged Pickett's Charge for my benefit.

All that took place actually was that Peggy Cass and I chatted with Col. Deane and a private, and Col. Deane briefly showed us the new Army rifle. We shot films of the wall which sealed off East Berlin, the Brandenburg Gate where just the day before an East Berliner had crashed through the barrier to freedom, and other points of interest.

Our interviews with a handful of soldiers consisted mostly of talk about their wives and babies. The conversation was about as provocative as the small talk at a P.T.A. meeting. There was no tension evident. In fact, while we were shooting, busloads of American G.I.'s were crossing into East Berlin on sight-seeing tours.

Across the border were a few bored, unarmed *Vopos* (People's Police) and a half dozen curious East German cameramen taking pictures of us taking pictures of them. The show ended with Peggy and me sitting alone on a curb in the rain. It was all decidedly unwarlike.

When I pointed out a water cannon across the border, and told Peggy it could knock a person down at 50 yards, she said, "I hope they won't use that. I just had my hair done."

That was the extent of the "incident" that both U.S. and Communist papers called "provocative." When the program was finally televised, showing on film exactly what had really taken place, it was generally admitted the whole thing was a tempest in a TV pot. The Senate Communications Subcommittee's watchdog said he could find nothing wrong with the show. Subcommittee staff director Nick Zaple added he saw no question raised involving broadcast regulation.

The morning after the program had been shown, the consensus was: "What was all the hullabaloo about?" There was an embarrassed silence from the most caustic critics but apologies from the more fair-minded papers and columnists.

"Anyone who saw the program," wrote the distinguished Washington columnist David Lawrence, "must have wondered why members of Congress who hadn't seen it, but had read newspaper accounts of the filming episode, went off the deep end in their criticism. In presenting worthwhile information *The Jack Paar Show* was an effective piece of work. He deserves not brickbats but applause for his revelation of the human story behind the Berlin crisis."

Columnist Paul Molloy of the *Chicago Sun-Times* felt that the programs were a restrained, low-key look at both sides of the wall. "The episodes showing actual escapes across the wall," he wrote, "and interviews with the escapees were among the most dramatic I have ever seen on television."

The *Chattanooga Times* was also among the papers conceding there was no wrong-doing on my part or the Army's. "Mr. Paar's actions at the border were above reproach," it editorialized. "So were the actions of the officers and men. The mild cooperation given to Mr. Paar appeared to be no different from that usually given the newsmen and others who are trying to present an accurate picture of the situation to the people back home."

The most gratifying aspect of the final outcome of the Berlin episode, as far as I was concerned, was not my personal vindication but the withdrawal of disciplinary action against Colonels Hoadley and Deane. The Army reinstated the two officers who had cooperated with us with the explanation that re-investigation showed that they had done nothing wrong. General Bruce C. Clarke, commander of the U.S. Army in Europe, said the reinstatement was made to "right an injustice."

I was disappointed that such a misleading uproar blew up around our show, as we tried very hard to bring American television viewers a clear picture of what the division of Berlin meant, in human terms, to the people on both sides of the border. I had done a program from Berlin just a year earlier, yet it still came as a shock to see again the enormous contrast between the gay, brightly lighted, prosperous, free Western sector, and the dreary, drab, Communist-held Eastern portion, with its miles of bombed-out areas and its unsmiling, dejected-looking captive people.

When Miriam, Randy and I walked down the Kurfurstendamm, the main street of West Berlin, with its dazzle of lights and chic shops, we felt an almost electric excitement. Yet strolling along Stalinallee, the main thoroughfare of the Eastern sector, was like stepping into the shadows. Even with its new, modern apartment houses, we could see miles of rubble just beyond them and I got the eerie feeling I was walking along a movie set for some B picture, with nothing behind the façade.

Flying over Berlin in a helicopter, I was amazed by its immense size. The total area of East and West Berlin together is nearly four times that of Washington, D. C., and the American sector of West Berlin alone is bigger than Paris.

On our first visit, the border between the divided cities was still open. Thousands of Berliners were crossing both ways every day, on the U-Bahn, the subway, the S-Bahn, an elevated railway, or by bus or streetcar. They were fleeing the East at the rate of several thousand a week even then.

On the first visit I interviewed Willy Brandt, the energetic, 46-year-old Mayor of West Berlin. Brandt, a charming, articulate man who speaks English beautifully, was one of the most impressive public figures I have ever met.

Despite Khrushchev's threats, the tousle-haired official seemed undaunted when I talked with him in his office, just a few hundred yards from the border of East Berlin. We spoke of the Russian threat to gobble up West Berlin by what he called "salami tactics"—a slice at a time—but he expressed confidence that the United States and its Western Allies would stand firm in their support of the West Berliners. He saw no quick or easy solution to the problem of divided Berlin and felt it would eventually be settled only as part of a general global settlement. Brandt did not seem to be unduly concerned by the possible outcome if Khrushchev did sign a separate treaty with East Germany.

"If Khrushchev wants to marry himself," he said, "let him do it."

Berlin was much changed when I visited it again a year later, just after the East Germans had sealed off the border. It did not seem as tense as I had expected, but infinitely more sad. Everywhere we heard stories of families separated by the 20-mile-long wall dividing the city.

I talked with escapees from East Berlin, including a family who had jumped out of their apartment building into a blanket held by friends on our side, and an 18-year-old *Vopo* who had leaped over the wall he was supposed to be guarding.

Despite the anxiety caused by the shutting down of the border, the people of West Berlin seemed generally optimistic and an atmosphere of *gemütlichkeit* prevailed. After dark, West Berlin becomes as lively as Birdland.

One night Peggy Cass and her husband went out with Tom Cochran, my associate producer. The waiter asked if they wished cocktails.

"Dry martini," Peggy answered.

"Dry martini," echoed her husband, Carl.

"Dry martini," added Tommy.

The waiter returned a moment later with *nine* martinis! That is how my friends discovered that *drei* in German means three!

I also got into a little incident involving drinking and German. One night I was having dinner with Paul Orr, my producer, at the Berlin Hilton, when I saw a woman approaching. From long experience my radar warned me that she was an American tourist bent on a long conversation with me.

"Why Jack Paar!" she greeted me.

Not wishing to interrupt our dinner, I looked up, shrugged, and said, "Nein."

The lady thought she was mistaken and apologized. Then she went back to a nearby table. I forgot about her and resumed talking English. She heard me and again came bearing down on us.

"I think it's an absolute disgrace," she fumed. "You stars come over here and get so drunk you don't even know who you are!"

After the lively night life of West Berlin, going into captive East Berlin is like waking up with a hangover after a gay evening. We drove through the Brandenburg Gate into East Berlin twice on our last visit and it seemed almost deserted, like a ghost city.

Even the modern buildings along Stalinallee seemed less than impressive. Some of the apartment houses, we were told, had transparent plastic pipes, so that if the residents didn't have TV they could at least sit around at night and watch the plumbing.

While the men in West Berlin were busy and prosperous looking, and the women the most chic and beautiful I have seen anywhere in the world, the people of East Berlin looked shabby and dejected.

We wandered over the grass-covered mound beneath which Hitler lay under the ruins of his "Thousand Year Reich," past the burned-out Reichstag and gutted churches. The once beautiful Unter den Linden looked bleak and deserted, and the Adlon Hotel, once one of the finest in the world, seemed forlorn and dilapidated.

East Berlin does have quite a thriving television industry. However, you get the feeling, as Bob Hope once said, that you don't watch it—it watches you.

Much of the East German programming is Soviet propaganda, though delivered by fetching-looking lady commentators who might tempt almost anyone to defect. I couldn't get the names of the programs in German, but they looked as though they might have been *This Is Your Life—Or Else* or *The Price Is Wrong*.

We also appeared on East Berlin television. The East Berliners had shot films of Peggy Cass and me doing our program from the Friedrichstrasse check point. However, they did not show it until a week after the incident when all the hoopla had appeared in the American press about it. Then they showed a one-minute film clip.

28

The Velvet Grindstone

FORGIVE ME if I seem to be running out of steam, but I've held the floor for quite some time now. As I write this final chapter of my second book I am approaching the end of my fifth year on the *The Jack Paar Show* and my fifteenth year of network broadcasting.

For more than four years I have been talking the better part of nine hours a week on the air. Before I'm through, in March, 1962, this stint will total thousands of hours of almost continual conversation, with time out for innumerable commercials and occasionally a little entertainment. If all those hours of conversation were laid end to end, I'm afraid they'd provide quite an earache.

Looking back over the seemingly endless conversations at midnight, I can't help but feel an overwhelming sense of relief that the ordeal is nearly over. The end is in sight at last, a release from days of living on my nerve ends and nights of sheer terror, going out before an audience of millions of viewers armed with nothing but a few notes. There never was a moment when I wasn't scared to death.

We've had our moments, though, and I feel we managed to shake things up occasionally and spread a little irreverence around. I believe we brought one valuable ingredient to television—strife, live and unrehearsed.

"We follow your program faithfully," a man in Michigan wrote, "and I want to thank you for the many wonderful fights you've brought into our home."

I've enjoyed tilting with windmills, and windbags, but now I'm weary and my saber is bent.

As I prepare to say farewell to the witching hours, it seems to me we created a kind of monument—a sort of Tower of Babel with commercials. In the course of doing so, I've met the most interesting people, as the saying goes. I've interviewed President Kennedy and a man who breaks boards in half with his index finger. I've talked with Dr. Tom Dooley and an English lady who hiked across the United States just for exercise. I've come to know Dr. Billy Graham, who told me that even I am not beyond the mercy of God.

I once introduced Dr. Graham to Max Asnas, the owner of the Stage Delicatessen. Max was so impressed at meeting the noted evangelist that he blurted, "Any friend of God's is a friend of mine."

I will claim no virtue for the program but one: it is genuine. I've never been anything but what I seemed, for better or worse, because I couldn't be if I tried. We've had our moments of laughter, these many past midnights, and occasionally of tears, and always they were real. Actors are a sentimental lot and I suppose I abuse the privilege.

I have been accused of being emotional and I admit it. I am so fond of some guests that I sometimes greet them on the show with as much enthusiasm as if they had just returned from a three-year expedition to the Gobi Desert.

I also have been known to shed a tear sometimes, on some touching occasion like the rare magic moments when, in a twinkling, talent and timing and audience empathy all came together to transform some unknown performer into a star.

On one such sentimental occasion everyone was embracing and otherwise celebrating and I shed a tear or two. In the midst of all this, I noticed John Lynch, our stage manager, who wears earphones and a mouthpiece, shying away from the emotional melée.

"What was wrong?" I asked him afterward. "You looked worried."

"I was afraid you might hug me while you were crying," John said, "and with all the electrical equipment I'm wearing we'd have been electrocuted!"

We've managed to do some useful things, too, though sometimes by accident. A veterinarian in Malibu, California, wrote me that he dozed off while watching our show and his house caught on fire. Then someone said something funny on the show and the audience howled so loudly that the man woke up, discovered the fire, and was able to save himself and his house.

I can't resist looking back with a certain ironic satisfaction as I near the end of my tenure on the show. When I started, people said I would never last because you had to "do something" to succeed on television and I didn't do anything but talk.

TV then was populated by acrobats, dog acts and people giving bird calls, and there was small demand for conversation. For a time, barking was more popular than talking. Now I'm trying to get *off* TV and the dog acts, acrobats and the rest are trying to get back *on*.

All my life in radio and television I was told I "wasn't commercial," yet I wound up on a show with more commercials than any other. I flunked arithmetic in high school but I'm on a program that grosses twenty million dollars a year. I hate to think of what might have happened if I'd *passed* arithmetic.

People find it hard to believe that I really mean to walk away from a show that is seen by thirty million viewers weekly, and earns twenty million dollars yearly, but I can hardly wait. I've seen what this pressure-cooker existence has done to some of my friends and I don't want it to happen to me. I feel that much more holding my nose to this velvet grindstone and they'd be getting out the wet sheets for me.

So what now? When I finish on the *Tonight* show I plan to do a new show once a week. But first I want to rest. I want to know my family better. I want to lie in bed longer. I want, just once, to read all the way through the Sunday papers.

I'll forget my cares and Dorothy Kilgallen. I'd like to travel. I'll go to places where no one wonders what Jack Paar is really like, and no one cares.

I'd like to do all the things I haven't done for so long. I can tell jokes about water closets with no one to interrupt me but my wife. I can stop and chat with someone on the street without wondering if he's a process server. I can sit at the worst tables in restaurants. Maybe I'll even get a listed telephone number. But don't call me.

I'll be out in the back yard cheating at croquet with Randy.

THE
GARFIELD
HONOR

The best-selling novel about a
ruthless Yankee who clawed his way
to luxury and power—and three
tempestuous beauties who
fought for the spoils

FRANK
YERBY

CARDINAL EDITION GC · 141/50¢

❖❖❖❖❖❖❖❖❖❖❖❖❖❖❖❖❖❖❖❖❖❖❖

Other novels by Frank Yerby

GC · 125/50¢	A WOMAN CALLED FANCY
GC · 150/50¢	CAPTAIN REBEL
C · 367/35¢	THE FOXES OF HARROW
GC · 109/50¢	GILLIAN
C · 400/35¢	PRIDE'S CASTLE
C · 352/35¢	THE SERPENT AND THE STAFF

❖❖❖❖❖❖❖❖❖❖❖❖❖❖❖❖❖❖❖❖❖❖❖

If your bookseller does not have these
titles, you may order them by sending re-
tail price, plus 5¢ for postage and handling
to: MAIL SERVICE DEPT., Pocket Books,
Inc., 1 West 39th St., N. Y. 18. Enclose
check or money order—do not send cash.

PUBLISHED BY 🄿🄱 POCKET BOOKS, INC.

For My Great Folly

A lusty, brawling novel
about seventeenth-century pirates

Thomas B. COSTAIN

PERMABOOK EDITION M•5051/50¢

*Other novels by
Thomas B. Costain...*

M•7501/75¢	THE BLACK ROSE
M•5029/50¢	THE DARKNESS AND THE DAWN
M•6001/60¢	HIGH TOWERS
M•7502/75¢	THE MONEYMAN
M•7505/75¢	RIDE WITH ME

PUBLISHED BY **pb** POCKET BOOKS, INC.